PREMIERE ELEMENTS MADE EASY

Turn Your Videos Into Movies

By James Bernstein

Bernstein, James
Premiere Elements Made Easy
Book 14 in the Computers Made Easy series

For more information on reproducing sections of this book or sales of this book,
go to **www.madeeasybookseries.com**

Contents

Introduction

Thanks to the invention of the smartphone, we can now record all the special moments of our lives, and even the not so special ones as I am sure you have seen if you have ever gone on a website such as YouTube or have an Instagram account! Of course smartphones are not the only device you can use to record video and many people still use video cameras to record things such as weddings, graduations and other special events.

One thing that is pretty common with people who record videos is that many times the video ends up being shown with all the footage that really doesn't need to be seen, or the video ends up not being seen at all because the person doesn't have the means to edit out all the unwanted footage to make a watchable video.

This is where using video editing software comes into play. When you have an easy way to edit and enhance your footage into something that others would enjoy watching, it makes the editing process fun and rewarding. Plus if you do it right, you can end up with a professional looking video that might even make you some money, or at least get you a bunch of clicks!

Adobe Premiere has been one of the most widely used video editing programs out there for many years and has some really advanced features that allow you to create some amazing videos. But if you are not a professional videographer then you might find this type of software to be intimidating and too complex to learn when it's not something you are doing as a career.

Adobe realized that there were people who had a need to edit their videos at home who were just doing it as a hobby and wanted something a little easier to use that was a bit more intuitive and that also didn't come with the huge cost that Premiere CC (Pro) comes with. So they released Premiere Elements way back in 2004 even though it really didn't start taking off until version 9 or so in 2010.

Premiere Elements is geared towards video editors who want to make great looking movies without having to get a degree in video editing. It has a much simpler interface yet still offers some advanced features to make your movies stand out.

The goal of this book is to get you comfortable using Premiere Elements without confusing and irritating you at the same time. I find that if you explain things like someone is a total beginner, even if they are not, it makes that topic much easier to understand, and that is the way this book was written—so that *anyone* can make sense of the content without feeling lost.

This book will cover a wide variety of topics such as the Premier interface, editing features, adding audio and images, using effects, exporting your videos and so on. This book will not be covering all the advanced Premiere features, but rather the essentials needed to get you familiar with the software and will show you what it takes to get your videos looking the way you want them to look. The examples I use will be based on the Premiere Elements 2020 version of the software, so if you have a different version, things might not look exactly the same, but you should still be able to follow along pretty easily.

So, on that note, let's import some videos and work towards winning that Oscar!

Chapter 1 – What is Premiere Elements?

Since you are reading this book, you most likely know what Premiere Elements is to some degree but may not know what kind of things you can do with this software. In order to use Elements properly, you need to know what it's capable of doing, otherwise you might be expecting too much from the software or you might even be underestimating the software.

Premiere Elements was designed for those who want an easy-to-use interface with step-by-step guidance that can produce results that look like they were done by a professional movie editor. They try their best to make the interface intuitive, so you don't get lost or frustrated trying to figure out how to perform even simple tasks.

Why Edit Your Videos?

If you have ever been on video sites such as YouTube you have most likely seen some well produced videos as well as some videos that look like they were put together by third graders. Then again you might also end up seeing some nicely done videos that were actually put together by third graders! The point I am trying to make is that if you plan on sharing your videos with others, you don't want them to be cringing on the inside while looking bored on the outside. The goal is to keep their attention and give them something enjoyable to watch.

If you have more than one video clip that you want to be part of a single movie then that will require some video editing on your part just to get that done. And if you want to edit out certain parts of your footage that you don't want to be seen then once again, that will require some editing. Plus of course you might want to do things like add music, images or effects to enhance your work.

Going back to the YouTube example, if you plan on uploading your videos to a site such as YouTube then you might want to make your videos a little more streaming friendly, so they work better with these online video sites. There are multiple ways to export your movies depending on what your final goals might be.

For the most part, raw footage doesn't make for exciting videos because you usually end up with a lot of footage you don't want to be included in the final movie and depending on the device you use to record the video you will often times need to make adjustments for things like audio levels, brightness, color and so on to get the desired results. Lucky for us, Premiere Elements makes this pretty easy and pretty painless.

What You Can Do with Premiere Elements
I mentioned in the previous section some of the things you can do to make your videos ready for their big "premiere" but wanted to go into a little more detail about what types of changes and improvements you can make using the software. And of course I will be going into more detail about these features throughout the book.

One of the most common things you will find yourself doing with Premiere is "fixing" your footage to improve the way it looks and sounds before exporting your final video. You can adjust things such as lighting, color, balance, volume, tone levels or use the Premiere auto fix features which will attempt to make the right changes for you. You can have the most exciting footage in the world but if you can't see it because it's too dark or the audio is overpowering then it's not going to make for a good video in the end.

Once you get your audio and video quality in check then you can work on things such as adding effects and transitions to your footage to spruce things up a bit and give your movies more of that "wow factor". Not only can you apply motion effects and do things such as fade in and out between scenes, but you can also apply custom transitions between your scenes and can also add effects to the video itself such as making the entire clip look like a cartoon with just a few clicks.

Many people like to add text to their videos to do things like describe what might be going on in a certain scene or to let the viewer now what location that part of the video was filmed at. There is even an option to add what they call motion titles which can be used as introductory parts to your video that have custom text and animated graphics.

I mentioned how you can add audio to your movies and Elements comes with a bunch of preinstalled music tracks that you can simply drag and drop into your movie and of course you can add your own music or sound effects just as easily.

When you are finally finished with your masterpiece then you can export it in various ways depending on what you plan on using it for. For example, you can export it to a DVD for watching on your TV, a high quality file for viewing on your computer and even as a video suitable for online streaming.

If this seems like a lot to take in then don't worry because I will be breaking everything down throughout the book and showing you some specific examples of how to perform all the tasks I will be discussing.

Premiere CC (Pro) vs. Premiere Elements
Since you are reading this book you have most likely bought Premiere Elements or are thinking about buying it. While you were shopping for the best price you might have noticed another version of the software called Premiere CC (Creative Cloud) or Premiere Professional as its often referred to. This is Adobe's serious version of Premiere made for those who edit videos for a living or are really into doing some professional level work.

Premiere CC also comes with a professional level price such as about $20 per month which adds up if you are only making movies every so often. This $20/month is a subscription to their "cloud" version of the software and that is the only way they offer it now.

On the other hand, you can get a copy of Premiere Elements for around $100 and even less if you are a teacher and have a school email address that you can use to make your purchase. Sometimes you can even find it for less online, but be wary of where you make your purchase to ensure you are getting legitimate software since you will most likely be downloading it from their site.

Once you buy Elements then that's it and there is no monthly fee to go along with it. You install it on your computer, register it and you are ready to go. But since it's not subscription based you will only be able to use the version you bought so when a new version comes out you will have to buy it again to upgrade. For the most part, you can skip a few versions when it comes time to upgrade because they are usually not different enough to justify spending the money unless there is a new feature that you must have. And if your current version does everything you need then there is no real reason to upgrade at all.

The way you work in Premiere CC vs. Premiere Elements varies quite a bit. Elements makes things much easier to accomplish by taking a lot of the manual steps out of various processes but at the same time you will lose some control of the process because of this. Premiere CC has many more tools that can be used to fine tune the editing process that are not included in Elements.

The editing interface is different as well with Elements being much more simplified which is a lot better for new users and those who just want to do the basics or use the built in tools and utilities that do much of the work for you. If you are new to video editing then you will probably find CC to be a bit overwhelming.

Photoshop CC will also support more video formats the Elements and if you have a professional quality camera then you might need to use CC in order to even import your footage. Plus CC will have more advanced exporting options that will need to be used for professional applications.

Chapter 2 – Premiere Elements Interface

Now it's time to dig into the software and take a look at everything you will be seeing when you open it for the first time. When you first open the software you most likely will see the Elements introductory screen as shown in figure 2.1. If you also decided to purchase Photoshop Elements then you will have an option to launch that from here as well by clicking on *Photo Editor*. Otherwise, you will click on *Video Editor* to launch Premiere Elements.

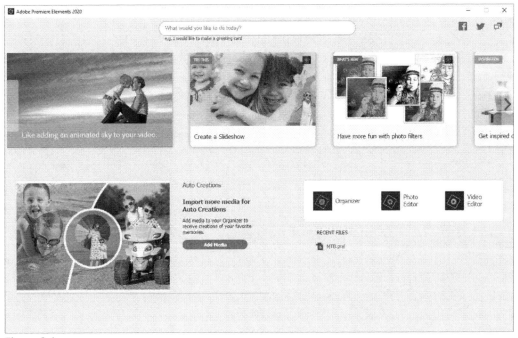

Figure 2.1

Once Elements opens you will see a screen similar to figure 2.2 which shows Premiere opened in *Quick Mode* which is usually the default mode when you open the software for the first time. You can see at the top of the screen that the word Quick is highlighted telling you that it is in fact in Quick Mode.

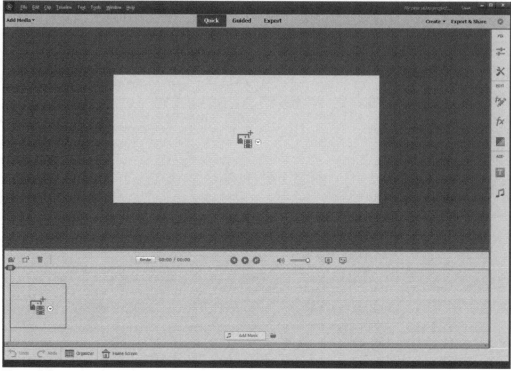

Figure 2.2

Workspace Modes - Quick, Guided and Expert

Speaking of modes, there are three different modes that you can work in while using Premiere Elements. These modes determine how the interface looks and what tools are available to you. The purpose of these modes is to offer you choices in the difficulty level of the software, so you don't get overwhelmed right from the start.

In my option the Expert mode is not really that complicated and is where you should really be working from, and is the mode I will be using throughout this book. Regardless, I will now go over each of these modes so you get an idea of what you can do from each one in case Expert mode is not for you.

Quick

This mode allows you to add one or more video clips into the timeline as well as add things like text and music with just a few clicks of the mouse. Figure 2.3 shows a project with two video clips added as well as a music file and some text and it took me about two minutes to get everything in there.

Figure 2.3

Figure 2.4 shows a closer view of the part of the workspace where I have my video and music files. You can see the two video files side by side and the music file that is called *Outer Space* beneath them. Take a look at all the buttons and the labels I gave to them and you will see how things are fairly self-explanatory when it comes to how the interface functions.

One of the great things about Premiere Elements is that you can add media and make your changes and then all you need to do is press the play button to see how it all fits together. Then if you need to change anything you can review the new results by clicking the play button once again. You can drag the red slider play bar to a specific point in the video to have it play from there if you don't want to watch the entire project from the beginning each time.

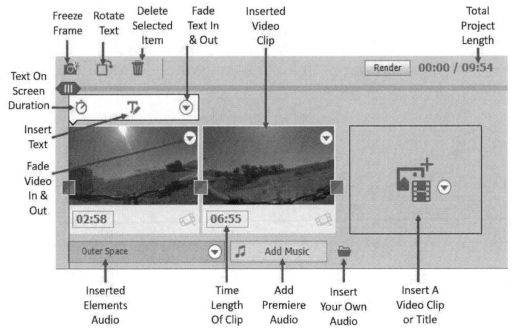

Figure 2.4

In order to effectively use Premiere Elements your computer hardware must meet a minimum performance level. If it doesn't then you will find that many tasks are painfully slow and that your video playback within Premiere will be very choppy and slow as well. Be sure to read up the minimum requirements for the software.

On the right hand side of the workspace, you will have almost all of the same Fix, Edit and Add options that you will have available in Expert Mode (figure 2.5). I will be going over each one of these groups of tools in Chapter 5.

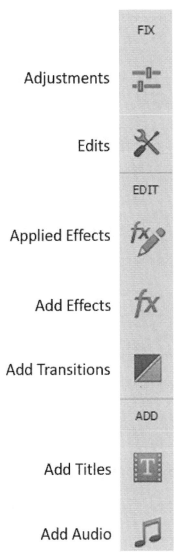

Figure 2.5

Guided

Guided mode can be used for those who want to be walked through the process of editing their videos step by step. You will still need to perform the steps, but the software will tell you exactly what you need to do based on what task you are trying to perform.

There are four categories to choose from (your version may vary) including *Basics* (figure 2.6), *Video Adjustments, Audio Adjustments* and *Fun Edits* (figure 2.7). The steps that you will be guided through will vary based on what task you are trying to perform.

Chapter 2 – Premiere Elements Interface

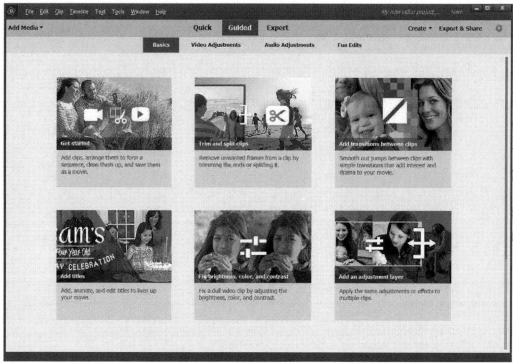

Figure 2.6

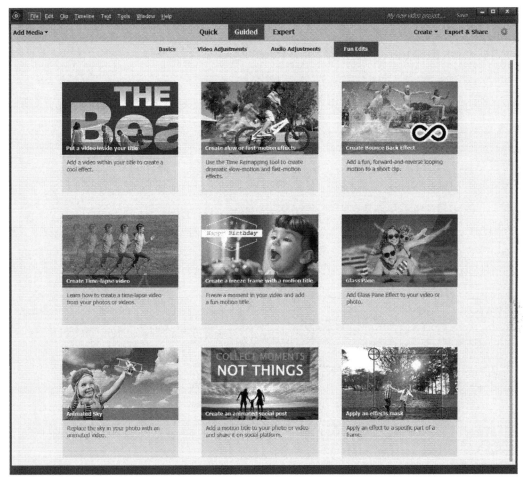

Figure 2.7

For my example, I am going to use the *Add transitions between clips* choice from the Basic group to add an animated transition effect between my two clips. Once I click on that box, Elements will take me into Expert Mode but show me exactly what I need to do in order to apply my transitions. Figure 2.8 shows the first step in the process and tells me exactly what I need to do. Notice how there are back and forward buttons making it easy to get the job done.

Figure 2.8

Once I click the next button, Premiere automatically opens up the Transitions choices allowing me to choose which type of transition I want to apply between my clips. It instructs me to drag the desired transition between the two clips on the timeline to have it applied.

Figure 2.9

Then it tells me that the process is complete and gives me a nice green checkmark to click on and that's all there is to it, at least when it comes to applying a transition between clips.

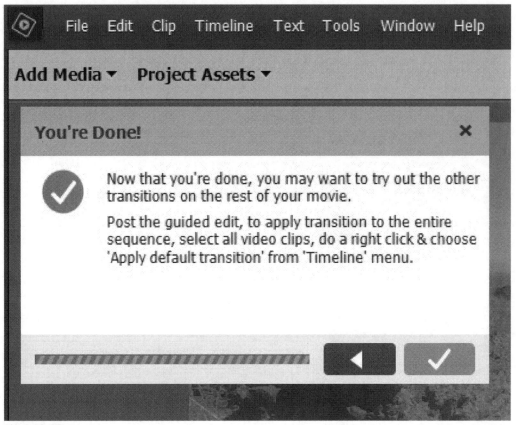

Figure 2.10

Expert

Finally, we have Expert Mode and as you can see from figure 2.11 it's not a whole lot different than Quick Mode except for how the timeline is displayed. It's more of an actual timeline rather than thumbnail previews of the project videos side by side. Since you will be spending most of your editing time in the timeline then I think it makes sense to have an actual timeline to work on.

I also think it makes it easier to get an overall view of all of the media (videos, audio, pictures, etc.) that you have imported into your project. As you read through this book you will get a better understanding of how the timeline works and eventually it will become second nature and I will actually be discussing the timeline in the next section.

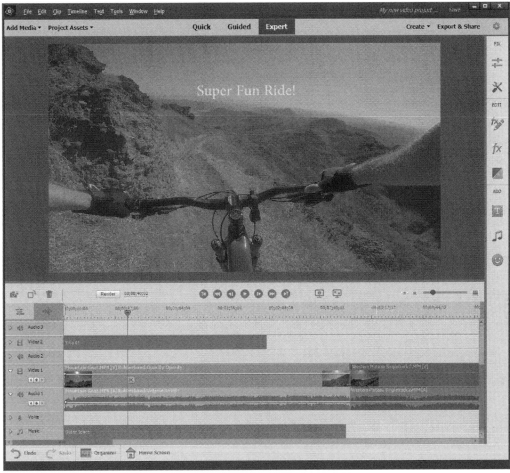

Figure 2.11

Elements Timeline

As I mentioned earlier, you will be spending most of your time in the Premiere timeline so it's important to know its components and how it works. Figure 2.12 shows the timeline for the project I have been working on throughout this chapter. As you can see I have two video clips, one title clip and one music clip.

The left side of the timeline shows the media categories such as video, audio, voice and music so you know what type of media clip you are working on. Premiere will also color code the clips making easier to tell them apart. If you look closely at figure 2.12 you will see that the video clips are broken into video and audio since my videos contain sound.

At the top of the timeline is the duration or length of your project. This comes in handy if you are concerned about your final video being a certain length.

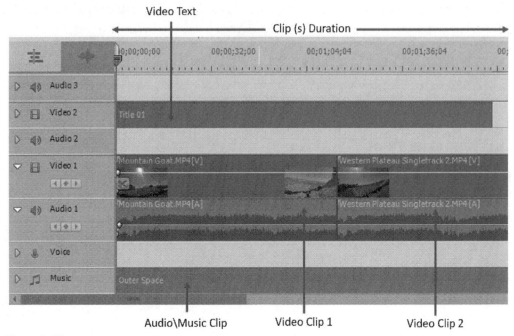

Figure 2.12

If you want to hide a video or audio clip from your project but not delete it then you can click the arrow next to that clip so it points downwards and then click on the film, speaker, microphone or speaker icon to put a slash line through it as shown for Video 1 in figure 2.13.

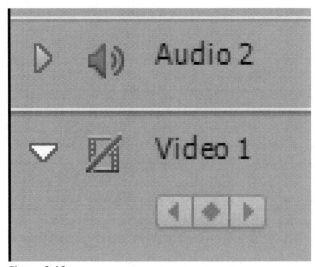

Figure 2.13

You can also drag your clips from one part of the timeline to another as long as it's the same type so you can drag the Title 01 text clip from Video 2 up to Video 3 for example if it helps keep you more organized.

Clicking on *Show Audio View* will change the way the timeline looks from the default *Classic View*. Then you will have options such as the ability to add your own narration to a track (red record button) assuming you have a microphone attached to your computer. Plus you can use the *Solo Track* option (headphones icon) to have only that audio be played within your project. You will also have a master volume level\meter on the right side of the timeline.

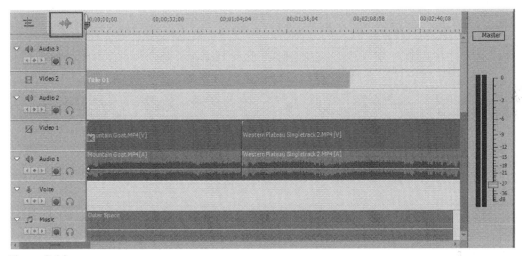

Figure 2.14

That covers the basics of the Elements timeline and as I get into my examples as I go along you will become more familiar with how to use the timeline.

Preview Screen

When making edits to your video, obviously it's important to be able to preview your work before you save it or export your video, and this is where the Preview Screen comes into play. You use this screen to view your current work to see how everything looks before you start to finalize your video production.

You have the typical controls that you are most likely used to such as play, rewind and fast forward and also have buttons that will take you back to your previous edit point and forward to your next edit point which makes it easy to see what changes you have made and alter them if needed. To the right of these buttons are options to have the playback take up the entire screen (full screen) and also options to change the playback quality and magnification.

Figure 2.15

When previewing your video you can drag the play position indicator slider anywhere on the timeline to move back and forth within your video (figure 2.16). That way you don't need to watch the entire video just to see the changes you made at a specific point in your project.

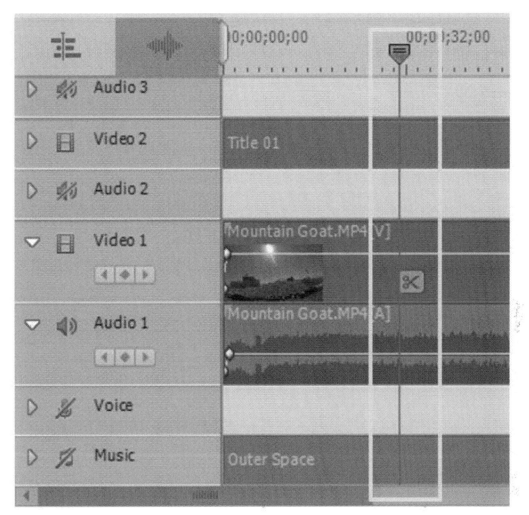

Figure 2.16

Project Assets
As you add media to your project you will start to notice that the number of videos, music clips, pictures and so on can start to grow and get out of hand but thankfully the Project Assets section can help you keep track of all of your files (figure 2.17). As you add media to your project, the files will get added to this section and then you can go here to manage these files. One thing to keep in mind is that you can have more items in your Project Assets than you do in use within your project. Just because you have a file here doesn't mean you have to use it within your project.

One quick way to add media to your Project Assets is to simply drag and drop the file from its location on your computer into a blank box in the Project Assets section. You can even drag it into the Preview Screen and Elements will add it to your assets.

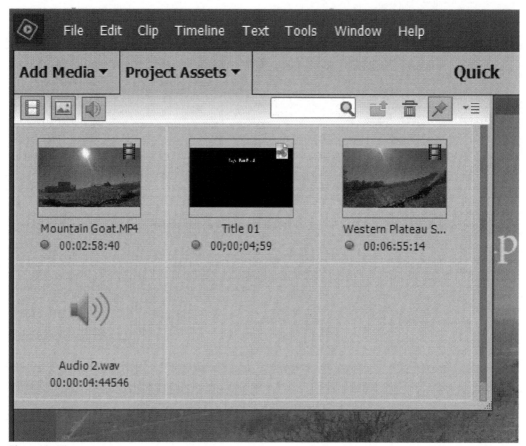

Figure 2.17

To use any of your media files with your project you can simply drag them from the Project Assets section into the timeline where you would like them to go.

Menu Items

At the top left of the Premiere Elements window, you will see the text menu items as shown in figure 2.18. There are many tools and options within these menus but many of them can be found in other sections of the workspace located on the right of the program and this is where you will most likely be accessing these tools and options from.

Figure 2.18

For now I will go over each menu item briefly and mention some of the more important selections rather than go over all of them. As I go along in this book I will be using these menus for specific tasks and will be going into more details about their functions.

File – Here you will find the typical items that you would in most software such as open, save, exit and so on. The most important selection here that we will be using later is the *Export and Share* option which is used to convert our project into a finished video ready for others to see.

Edit – The Edit menu also has some familiar commands such as cut, copy and paste as well as undo and redo. If you want to adjust your project settings or your preferences then you will find those options here.

Clip – Here is where you can go if you need to make adjustments to specific clips within your project. Things you can do here include disabling clips, renaming clips, ungrouping audio and video as well as changing video and audio options.

Timeline – From here you can do things such as zoom in and out on the timeline, set timeline markers, add tracks and render your work area which is an important step to take before exporting your video.

Text – If you plan on adding any text to your video and need to make changes to that text then this is the place to do so. You can do things such as change the type size, text alignment and orientation as well as its position and size within the video.

Tools – The Tools menu item contains various tools (obviously) such as an audio mixer and menu maker. It is also a place where you can go to launch guided utilities such as the Candid Moments feature that will try to extract still images from your video that you can save as image files.

Window – The Window menu is a little different than the typical Window menu you would see on other programs. Here you can do things such as view your project assets and add media as well as view your work history and applied effects.

Help – Today's Help menus are not like they were in the past where the software had a built in help interface that you could search to find answers to your questions. Nowadays they typically take you to a website where you can hopefully find the answers you are looking for. The Help menu for Premiere also gives you options to watch training videos or participate in the Premiere online forum where you can talk to other people about the software.

Premiere Preferences

For most people, the default Premiere configuration and settings should work just fine but if you are the type who likes to tweak your software and see how things work under the hood then you can take a look at the preferences section and see if there is anything you could benefit from by changing.

There are many upon many settings that you can change in the configuration but to keep things simple I will go over the more commonly changed settings and the ones that I find to be the most useful. To get to the preferences simply click on the *Edit* menu and then click *Preferences* and choose the section you wish to modify.

The first section I want to discuss is the *Audio Hardware* settings. You most likely won't need to change anything here but if you have more than one audio device such as an external sound device or a microphone that you want to use to add narration to your video then you can tell Premiere which device to use for what purpose from here. It's also a great place to come and check if you are having sound interface issues.

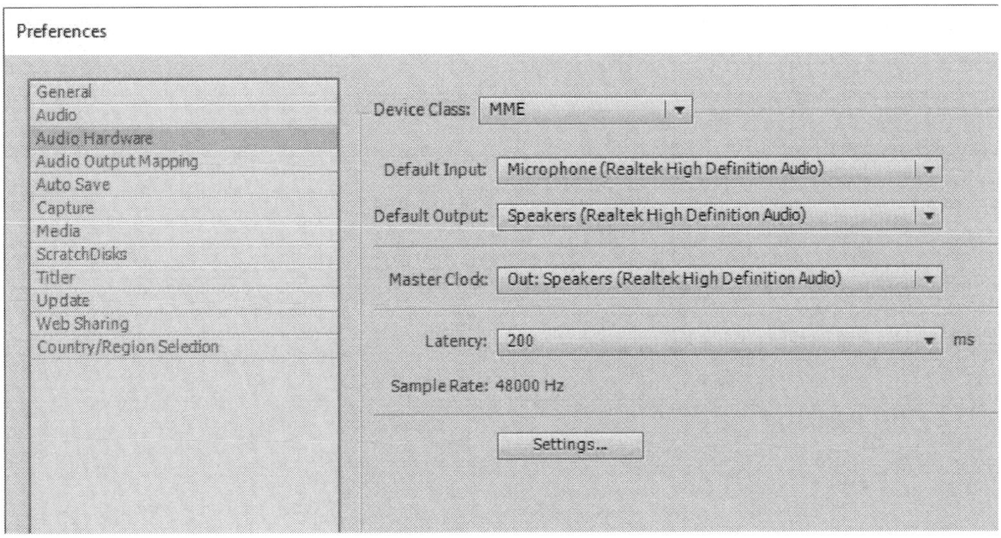

Figure 2.19

Next, the *Auto Save* settings which are used to automatically save your work at specified periods of time in case you are the type that forgets to do so. This way if your computer or Premiere crashes in the middle of you working on your project you can recover your saved work back to the last save point. The default time interval that Premiere saves your work is every 15 minutes. You can also turn off this feature if desired.

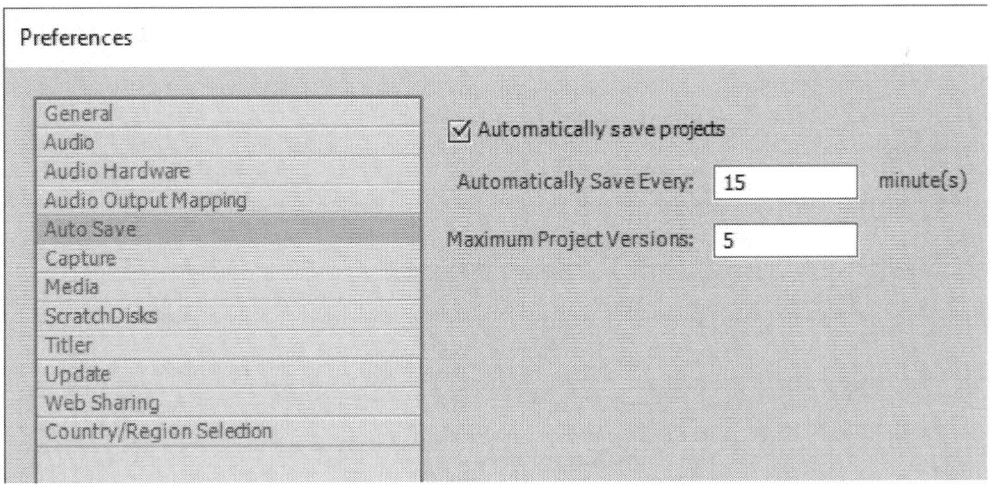

Figure 2.20

The *Media* section is important because this tells Premiere where to save things such as temporary and cache files while you are working on your video. The default location is *C:\Users\YourUsername\AppData\Roaming\Adobe* but you can change that to a different folder or drive in case you are low on storage space and have a bigger drive that you want to use.

If you need to get some space back on your hard drive you can click on the *Clean Now* button to have Premiere clear out the cache files to free up some space. There is also a checkbox that says *Automatically Clean Once in a Month* that is checked by default which will do this process for you once a month.

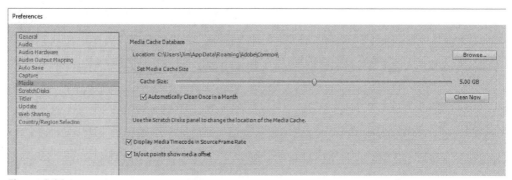

Figure 2.21

The *ScratchDisks* section is similar to the Media section because it's the location that Premiere uses to keep files that it needs for your projects as you are working on them. The types of files it stores here can be video previews, captured audio, project auto-save files and so on. Once again you can change the storage location for the various types of files if you have a different location that works better.

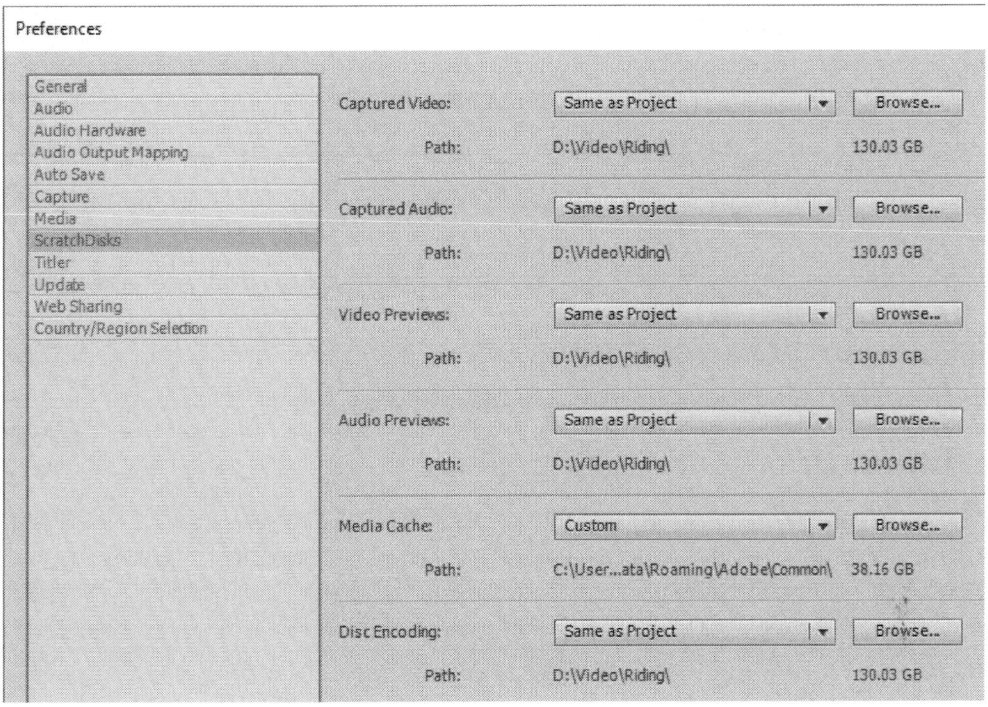

Figure 2.22

Feel free to check out the other sections in the Preferences to see if there is anything you might want to change to make the software work better for you.

Chapter 3 – Starting the Editing Process

Now that we have the boring stuff out of the way it's time to start working on making some movie magic. Or at least try to make a video that someone might want to watch! Of course, we will need to have some video to edit and have an idea of what we want to do with that video before we can actually get started.

Creating a New Project

The first step in the editing process is to create what Premiere calls a project. A project is a collection of videos and audio that you have in one file that you can then manipulate to create your final video file.

To start a new project simply go to the *File* menu and click on *New* and then choose *Project*. You will then be prompted to enter a name for your project and select where you want to save the file. You can either choose the default location that Premiere uses or you can click the *Browse* button to choose a location of your own.

New Project				×
Name:	Bike Trip			
Save In:	D:\Cool Video	▼	Browse...	
Project Settings:	NTSC-AVCHD-Full HD 1080i 30			
	Change Settings...	OK	Cancel	Help
	☐ Force selected Project Setting on this project			

Figure 3.1

It is always a good idea to know what type of video file you are working with so you can choose the proper project settings to match your file details as closely as possible. That way you can click the *Change Settings* button and then choose your options based on that information. For Windows users, you can right click your video file and choose *Properties* to get this information. On the *Details* tab, you will see things such as the width, height and frames per second for your video. Figure 3.2 shows that I have an MP4 video file that is 1920x1080 (1080p) and is 30 frames per second. It also shows information for the audio properties but that is not as critical to know as the video details.

Figure 3.2

Now when I click on the Change Settings button I will see all the many options I have to choose from for my project (figure 3.3). The main thing you will need to choose first is either NTSC (National Television Standards Committee) or PAL (Phase Alternating Line) and then choose a setting within the proper category. If you are in the United States then you will most likely choose NTSC and if you are in Europe you would use PAL.

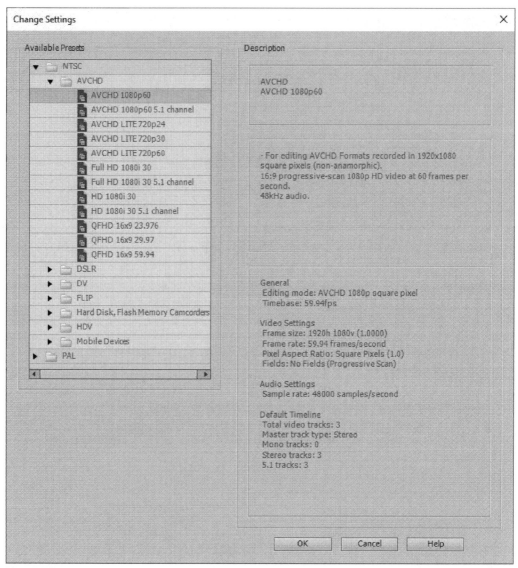

Figure 3.3

I can't tell you which setting to use because it will vary based on the camera you used to record on but if you click on a setting it will give you some information about that can help you make your decision as shown in figure 3.4.

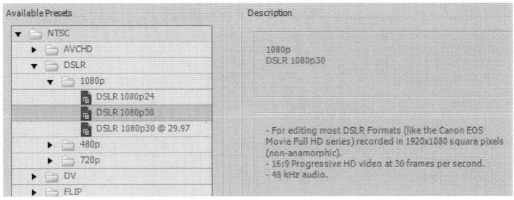

Figure 3.4

If you look back at figure 3.1 you will see a checkbox *labeled Force selected Project Setting on this project*. If you leave that box *unchecked* the Premiere will do its best to use its own settings that best match your files. So if you are not sure what settings to use then you can simply click *OK* at the New Project dialog box and have Premiere choose the settings for you.

Transferring Videos from Your Camera to Elements
Since the main reason to use Elements is to edit your videos you obviously need to get your videos into the software so you can start working on them. There are a couple of different ways to do this and whatever way you choose to use will work just fine.

At the top left of the screen, you will see an option that says Add Media (figure 3.5) and from there you have some choices as to where you can add your video and audio files from. This will also work for photos that you want to add to your project. You can also get to these same import options from the file menu as shown in figure 3.6.

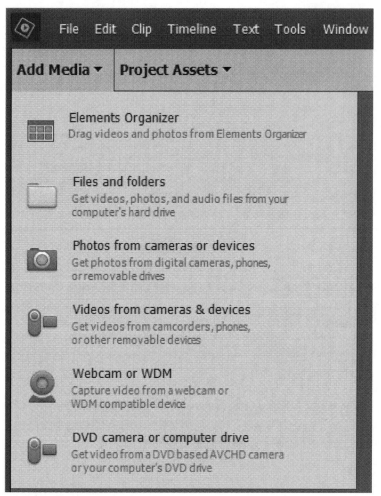

Figure 3.5

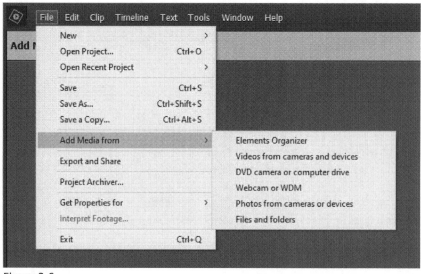

Figure 3.6

The method you will use will depend on where your media files are located. For example, if you have them stored on the hard drive of your computer you would use the *Files and folders* option to then browse to the location of your files and import them from there.

If you want to import the media right from your camera or smartphone you would use the *Videos from cameras & devices* for video files or *Photos from cameras and devices* for photos (discussed next).

Figure 3.7 shows how the interface looks when I use the *Videos from cameras & devices* option with my GoPro camera connected to my computer. It finds the video files located on my camera and then gives me the option to choose which ones I want to import into my project and where I want to save the files that it imports. Plus I can choose to have the files added to my timeline right away by clicking the box that says *Add To Timeline* or I can add them manually later on.

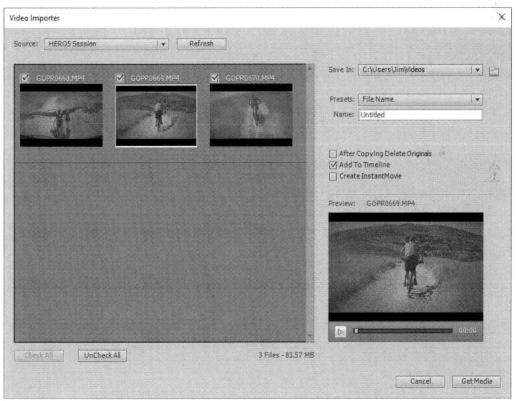

Figure 3.7

 I like to create a folder on my computer that is used to store all the media files for my project, so they are easier to keep track of. This way I can just copy the files from my camera and put it aside so it's out of the way and also so I can remove the files from the camera in case I need room for more.

The *Elements Organizer* is an additional component that comes with Premiere Elements and Photoshop Elements that allows you to organize all of your pictures and movies and do things like create albums and so on. I am not a fan of this program and find it tedious to use but you can try it out and see how you like it. Regardless, if you do use the Organizer you can add media to your project from there as well.

Figure 3.8

Another method that can be used to add media to your project is to open the *Project Assets* section and drag and drop files from your computer right into the individual boxes. Figure 3.9 shows how the Project Assets area looks when there are no files and figure 3.10 shows how it looks after I added two videos, an MP3 music file and a photograph.

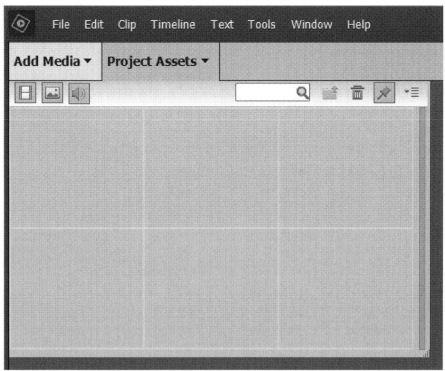

Figure 3.9

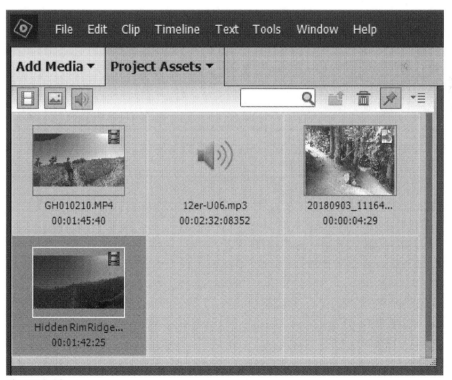

Figure 3.10

You can also drag and drop files right on to the timeline and they will be added to your Project Assets and placed on the timeline at the same time.

Transferring Pictures from Your Phone to Elements

If you are like most people, you use your smartphone as your camera rather than using something like a digital camera or even a camera that uses film (remember those?). Most smartphones actually take better pictures than the digital cameras we used just a few years ago!

In order to import the photos you have taken with your phone, you will need to either put them on your computer first which is what I like to do, or you can add them directly from your phone to your project. Sure, you can email them to yourself like many people do but if they are high resolution photos, then your email app may reduce the size in order to email them, leaving you with a lower quality picture by the time you get it from your email on your computer. Or, if you try to email them full size, you might get stuck only being able to attach one or two to an email and end up having to send a bunch of emails to yourself if you have a lot of pictures you want to put on your computer.

The best way to get your pictures off of your phone is to connect your USB cable from your phone to your computer and copy them over that way. The process for doing this varies from phone to phone and model to model, so you may have to research how to do this process on your phone if you need help.

Depending on what model of phone you have, when you connect your smartphone to your computer, a few different things might happen. If it's the first time you have connected it to your computer, it may take Windows or MAC OS a while to recognize your phone. Then you may or may not get a window that pops up showing the folders contained on your phone's internal storage. Some Android phones, for example, make you pull down a menu from the notification area that has connectivity options such as "transfer files" or "charge the phone only". iPhones will typically pop up a message asking if you want to trust this computer, and you have to confirm that before it will let you access the phone's storage from your computer. Once you get into the phone's storage, you will typically want to look for a folder that is called "DCIM", which will have your pictures stored in it. Once you open this folder, you can drag and drop the files onto the desktop of your computer, or into another folder of your liking. From there you can then add them to your Project Assets like you do with videos.

If you would rather have Premiere access your phone and add the pictures to your project that way then you can use the *Photos from cameras and devices* from the Add Media section. Next, you will need to select your phone from the *Get photos from* dropdown selector.

Figure 3.11

Under *Import Settings* you can choose where Premiere downloads the photo files too and if you want subfolders to be created based on attributes such as the shot date or a custom name that you choose.

Once you choose your device from the list you will then need to select what folder on your phone you want to import the photos from. In most cases, it will be the DCIM folder like I just discussed. Then Premiere will download the files from that folder to your computer to be used in your project.

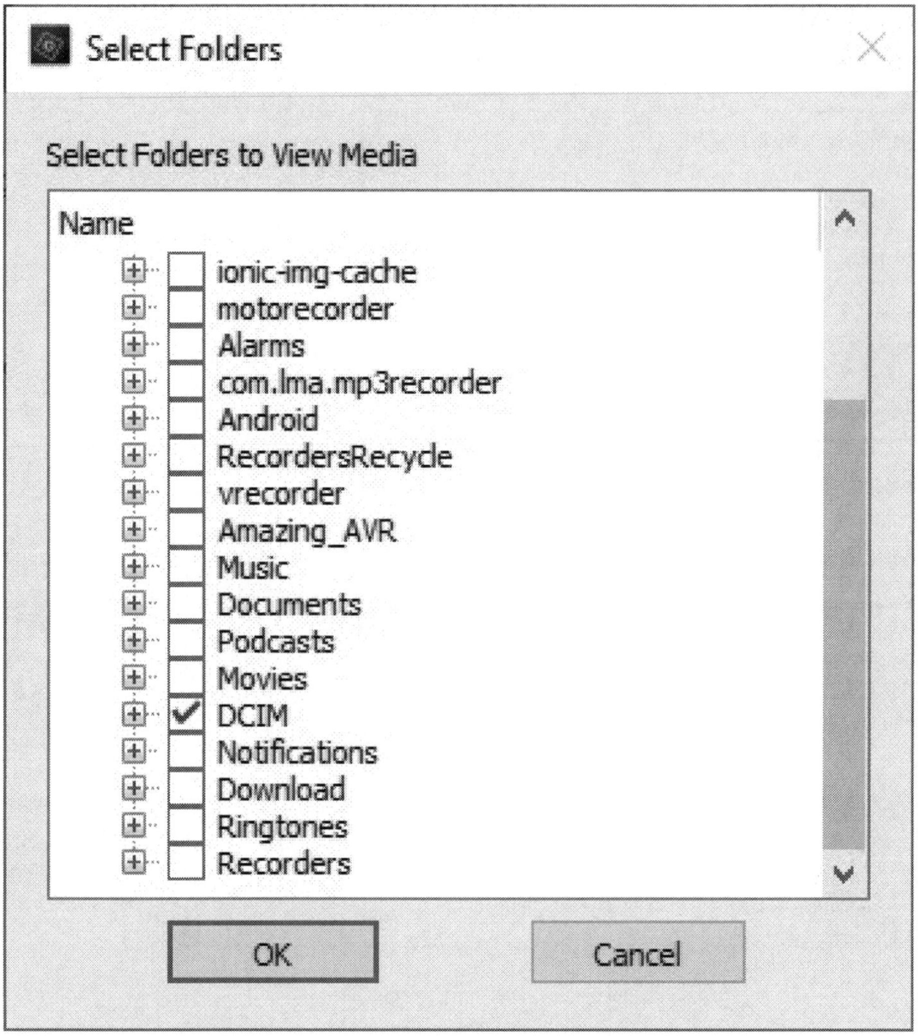

Figure 3.12

If you click on the *Advanced Dialog* button you will be able to see what photos you have on your phone and have more control over which photos will be transferred to your computer.

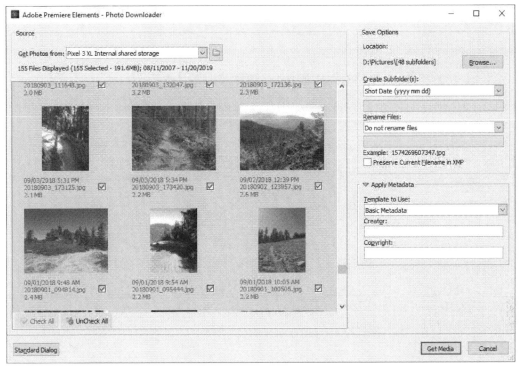

Figure 3.13

Once you click on the *Get Media* button then the pictures you chose will be added to your Premiere project and will ready for you to then add to your video. I will be discussing how to add images to your videos in the next section.

Adding Videos, Music and Images to the Timeline

Now that you have your videos etc. in your Project Assets group it's time to add them to the timeline so you can start making your edits. If you remember the breakdown I did of the timeline back in Chapter 2 you will remember (hopefully) that there are specific sections of the timeline made for specific types of media. To refresh your memory I have added the timeline graphic from that chapter below.

As you can see on the left of the timeline there are labels for the particular types of media that you can add to your timeline. To add a video, audio file or picture to the timeline, simply drag it from your Project Assets to the corresponding section of the timeline. These sections are referred to as Tracks by the way.

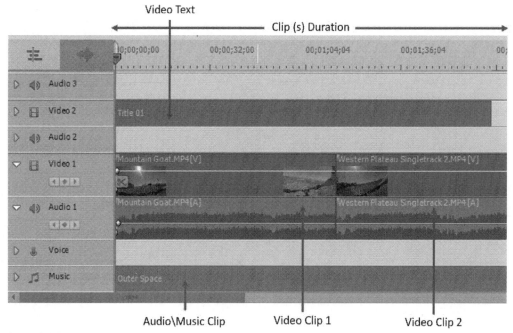

Figure 3.14

There will be multiple tracks for the same type of media in case you need to have overlapping media files. For example, you might want some sound effects playing in the background of your video but also have some narration being played at the same time. If so you can have two different audio tracks that play at the same time in the video.

If you need to add another track to your timeline you can simply go to the *Timeline* menu and choose *Add Tracks* and choose what type of track you want to add and where you want it to go.

Add Tracks		✕

Video Tracks

Add: 1

Placement: After Last Track ▼

OK

Cancel

Audio Tracks

Add: 1

Placement: After Last Track ▼

Figure 3.15

If you end up with a lot of media files in your project and are having trouble keeping track of them during the editing process you can rename the tracks by right clicking on the one you want to rename and choosing *Rename*. As you can see in figure 3.16 I renamed my video and my music tracks so they make more sense to me.

Figure 3.16

You can also drag and drop your media clips from one track to another if you want to rearrange and organize them. Just keep in mind that they will need to be the same track type such as video to video or audio to audio.

Using the Create Options

Now I would like to switch gears for a minute and discuss one of the features of Premiere Elements that is designed to help you make great looking video without too much work or editing skills involved. At the top right hand corner of the screen, you will see a *Create* option with a down arrow that you can click to select one of the three categories you can choose from to help you quickly create a professional looking video.

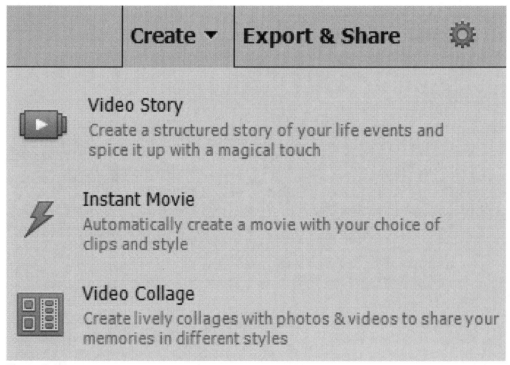

Figure 3.17

I will now go over each one of these categories and show you what you can do with them. Well, I will try my best since you can't watch videos while reading a book!

Video Story

Video Stories are used to tell a story about a certain event by using videos, text and animations based on a specific category. When you choose this option, Premiere will give you several categories to choose from that have built in templates that are used to create your story.

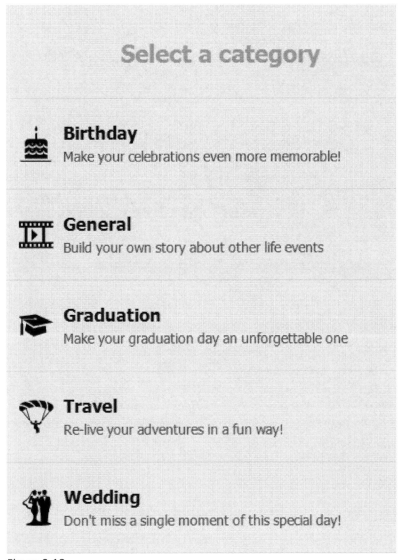

Figure 3.18

I'm going to choose the Travel option and then Premiere suggests the Travel Dairies story even though I can scroll through other stories if I don't think this one applies to my video. If you take a look at figure 3.19 you will see a checkbox that says *Use the original video clip from my timeline*. If you check this box then it will use the videos that you have already added to your timeline, otherwise you will be starting from scratch which is what I am going to do.

Figure 3.19

The first time you use a particular story it will have to download the content for that story off the Internet so in case you are wondering what is going on after you click on *Get Started*, that is what it is doing.

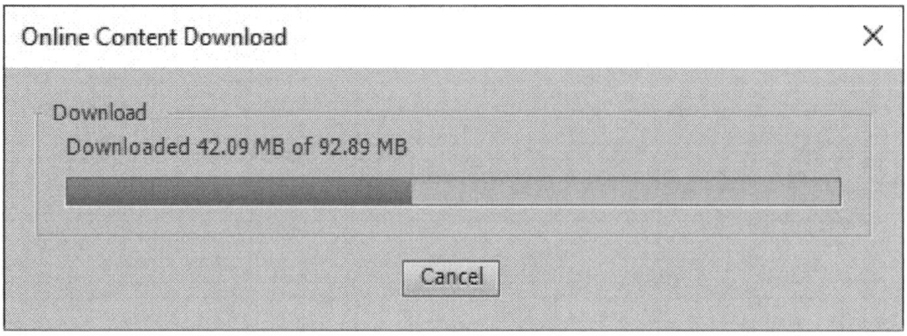

Figure 3.20

Next, you will need to drag and drop any photos or videos that you want included in your story. You can do this using the same methods that I went over earlier in the chapter. You can't insert any audio or music files though.

Story Assets

Drag & drop the photos and videos you would like to include in your story

When you're done, click 'Next'

Figure 3.21

Figure 3.22 shows that I have two video files and one photo added to my story and when I'm ready to continue I will click on the Next button.

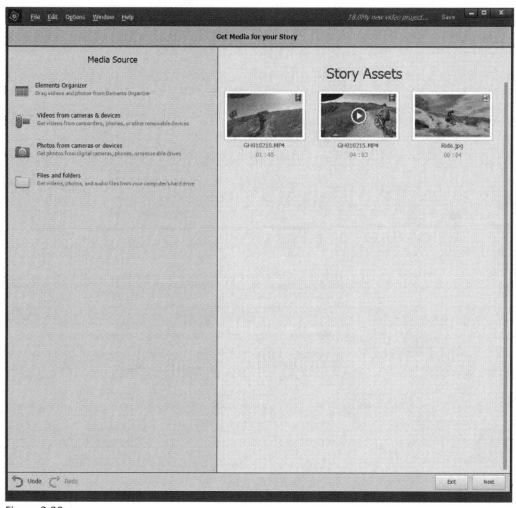

Figure 3.22

Next, you will take the media files that you added to the story and place them at the appropriate places within the predetermined chapters that come included with that particular story. You might find that there are more chapters than you have media for so if you want to remove one or more you can simply click on *Hide* or *Delete* Chapter, so it won't be shown. You can also add more chapters if needed.

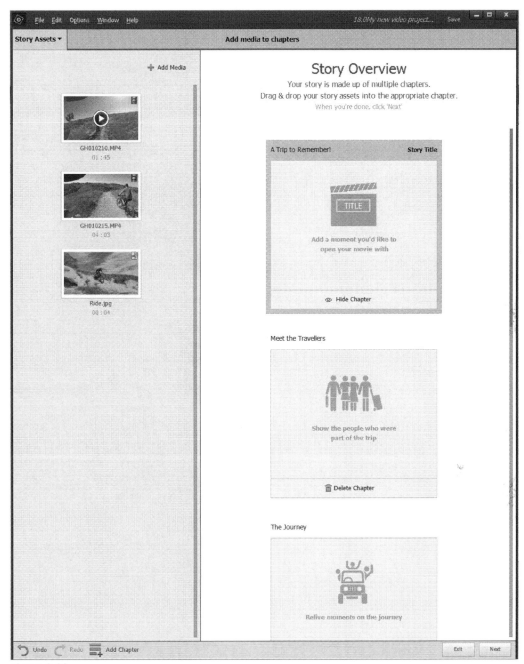

Figure 3.23

Figure 3.24 shows how it looks after I added my photo and two videos to my story. This story and my associated media don't really go together but I just wanted to show you how a story template looks rather than use a blank one which would be better suited for my videos.

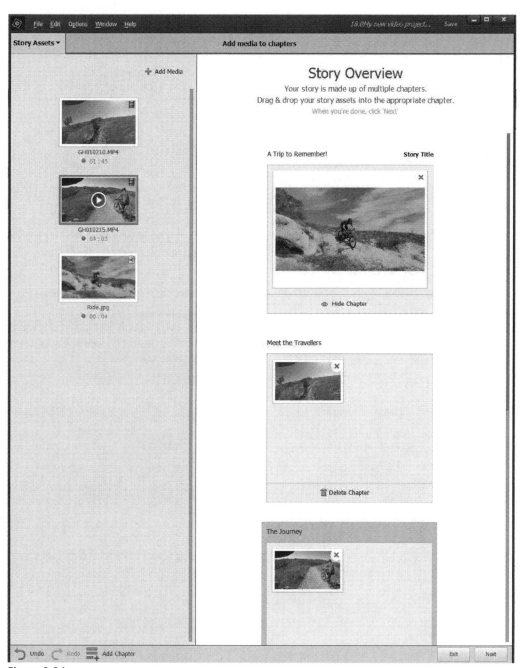

Figure 3.24

When you click on *Next* it will take you to a screen where you can see all of your chapters (figure 3.25) and preview each one by clicking on them (figure 3.26). You can also change the *Story Title* if desired by typing in a new one.

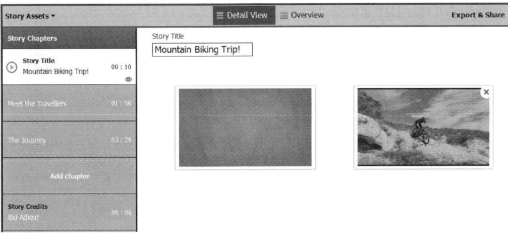

Figure 3.25

Figure 3.26

When you have everything looking the way you like you can click on the *Preview* button at the bottom of the screen to see how your movie will look. Then if you like what you see, you can click on the *Export to Timeline* button to have your story set up for you within the Premiere timeline. You will then be prompted to save the project to your computer first.

If you ever find that your video previews are slow or choppy then it is most likely because your video files have not been rendered within Premiere. Rendering takes all of your media and puts it together into one clip making it all run together smoothly. Rendering will be discussed in Chapter 6.

Finally you will see all of the media inserted for you on your timeline (figure 3.27) and you can then export your video story (discussed in Chapter 6) or make additional editing changes on the timeline itself.

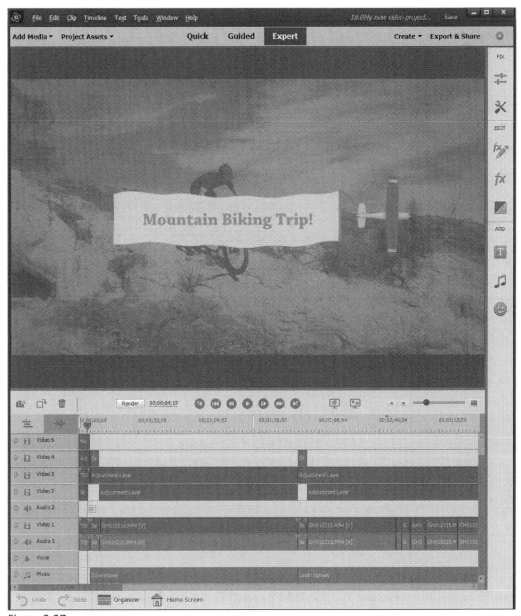

Figure 3.27

Instant Movie
This option can be used to turn your clips into a movie complete with music and special effects based on the theme that you choose. To use the Instant Movie feature you need to have at least one clip already present on your timeline. Then you can choose the theme that best fits the movie you are trying to create.

Figure 3.28

Once you choose a theme, Premiere will download the movie template files and load them into your copy of the software. These files can be on the large side so it might take a few minutes to complete. After the download is complete you will be asked to personalize your movie as shown in figure 3.29. I expanded some of the sections so you can get an idea of the things you can adjust. I also changed the default Opening Title and Closing Title.

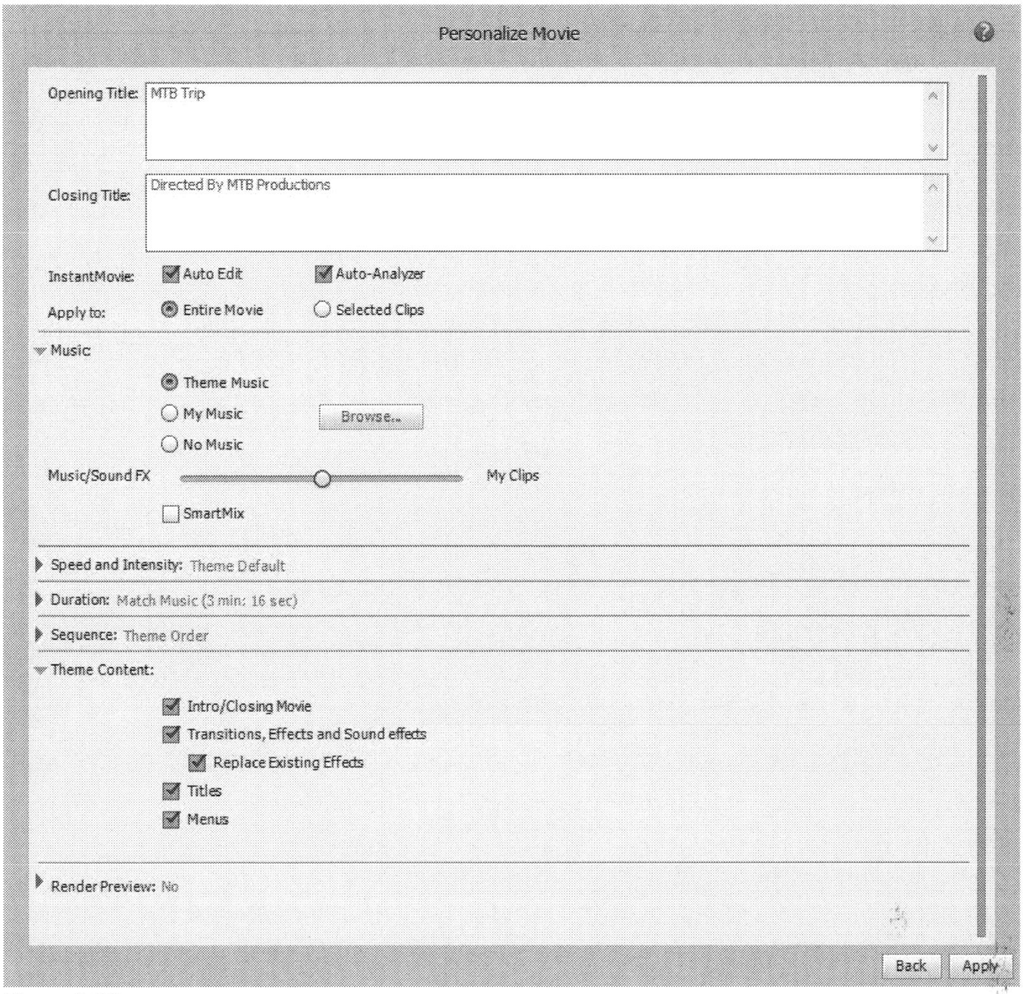

Figure 3.29

When you click on Apply you will get a message telling you that this theme will replace any effects that you have applied in your project with its own.

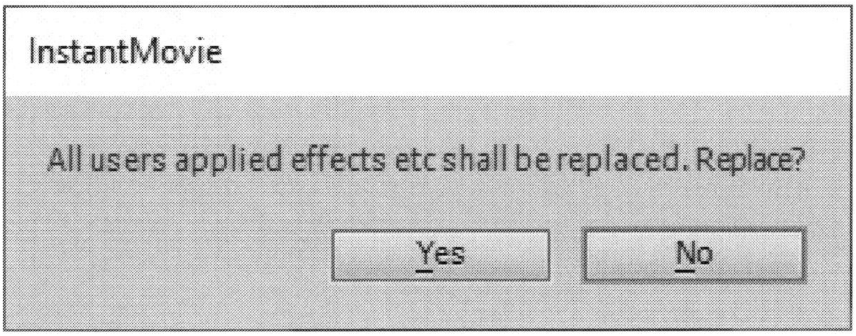

Figure 3.30

Premiere will then analyze the video clips that you have in your timeline.

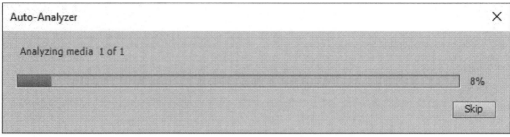

Figure 3.31

Next, it will tell you that it recommends rendering your footage which is a good thing to do in order to have your preview playback run smoothly.

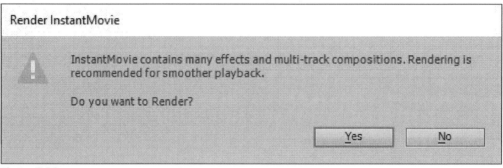

Figure 3.32

Obviously, I can't play the movie to show you the results but figures 3.33 through 3.36 show some screenshots of the effects that Premiere added to my Instant Movie, and it also added some custom transitions between scenes as well as its own music soundtrack.

Figure 3.33

Figure 3.34

Figure 3.35

Figure 3.36

If everything looks good then you can export your new Instant Movie just like you can with any other footage you have edited within the timeline.

Video Collage
Finally, we have the Video Collage choice which lets you make a collage out of various video clips and also add music to your movie. The first thing you need to

60

do is choose a template which determines how the videos will be laid out in your collage. Figure 3.37 shows the template configuration that I will be using for my collage.

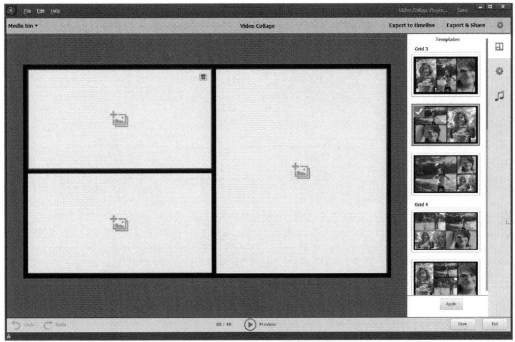

Figure 3.37

Next, you can choose a playback order such as one after another or all together. If they are short clips then one after another is probably the way to go but if they are all long clips or all the clips are approximately the same length then you might want to use the *all together* option.

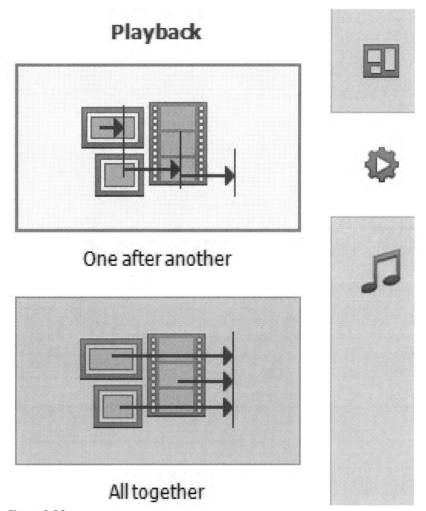

Figure 3.38

Next, you can choose your background music (optional) from the available choices that come with Premiere and once again the music will need to be downloaded to your software when using it the first time.

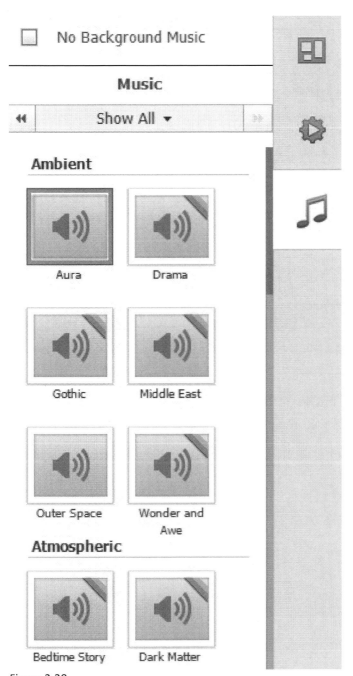

Figure 3.39

You will need to add your videos or pictures to your collage and then drag them to the appropriate space in the project. You can do this when choosing your template or do it at the end before you create the slideshow. This time I will make a dog video using some dog video clips I have on my computer.

Figure 3.40

You can then click on the Preview button to see how everything will look and sound with all of your configurations.

Figure 3.40

If things are looking the way you like you can then click the *Render* button to have Premiere finalize your collage or you can click on *Export to timeline* so have all the clips, music and effects put on your timeline for further editing or exporting. After you export it to your timeline simply click on the *Exit* button and you will be brought to the timeline with your collage media on the timeline and ready to go.

Chapter 4 - Basic Premiere Tasks

Once you decide on what video clips, audio clips, music and pictures you want to add to your final movie it is then time to start the real work once you get everything in place and imported into Premiere.

Once you get the basic editing processes down you can then move on to more advanced editing features to make some really professional looking movies. But if you don't get the basics down, then you won't even have a movie worthy of exporting and we definitely don't want that!

Managing Project Assets

I talked about importing your media into Premiere in the last chapter but wanted to take a moment to go over managing your media so you know where your videos etc. are located and can keep track of things so your project doesn't turn in an unorganized mess of clips.

Figure 4.1 shows the project assets for my current project. I have one image file, two video files and one music file. If you look at the file extension for each one, that will tell you what type of file each one is. For example, the first one called Ride.jpg has **.jpg** for the file extension which is used for image files. I also have two .MP4 files which are used for videos along with .avi, .wmv and so on. For my song file, I am using an MP3 file that you most likely have heard of.

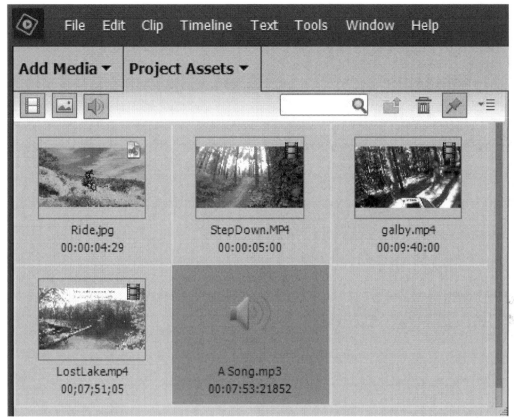

Figure 4.1

File extensions are used to tell your operating system (Windows, Mac OS, etc.) what program to open a certain type of file with. If they weren't used, then every time you double clicked a file you would be asked what program you wanted to open it with, and if you didn't know what type of file it was, then that would make things very difficult. File extensions are hidden by default in Windows (with a few exceptions). A file extension consists of a period followed by three or more letters (or sometimes numbers) afterward denoting what program the file is to be associated with. For example, with a file called **resume.docx,** the file name is **resume** and the extension is **.docx,** and **.docx** is the file extension associated with Microsoft Word. So, when you double click the resume.docx file, Windows knows to open it with Microsoft Word. However, if you don't have Microsoft Word installed, it won't know what to open it with because Word will register that extension with Windows only after you install it on the computer.

Right clicking on one of your project assets will give you several options as to what you can do with them. Cut, Copy, Paste, Clear, Rename and Duplicate should be pretty obvious, but I want to go over some of the other options available from this list that you might find useful.

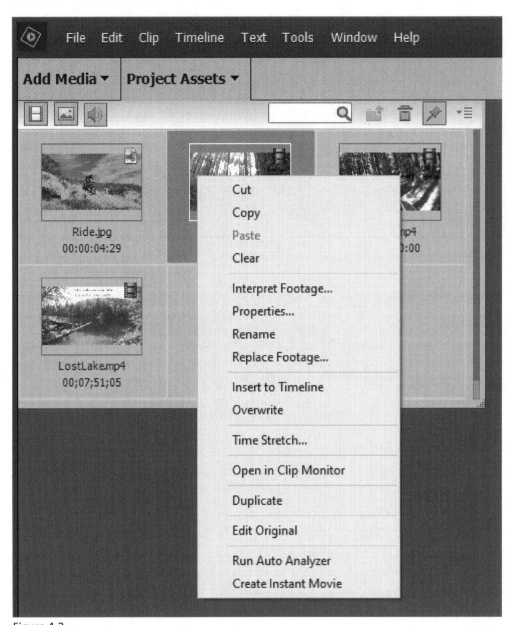

Figure 4.2

Properties

Checking the properties of one of your assets is more informational than anything in case you need to compare a couple of clips with each other to check things like the video size or frame rate.

Properties

File Path: D:\Video\Riding\WA Rides\StepDown.MP4
Type: MPEG Movie
File Size: 5.37 MB
Image Size: 1280 x 720
Frame Rate: 29.97
Source Audio Format: 48000 Hz - compressed - Stereo
Project Audio Format: 48000 Hz - 32 bit floating point - Stereo
Total Duration: 00:00:05:00
Pixel Aspect Ratio: 1.0
Alpha: None
Video Codec Type: MP4/MOV H.264 4:2:0

Figure 4.3

Replace Footage will allow you to replace that particular clip with another one from your computer by browsing to the location of the media file.

Insert to Timeline will place that clip within the timeline but I find it easier just to drag and drop it into the timeline where I would like it to go.

Overwrite will take this particular clip and overwrite whatever clip you have highlighted on your timeline making it easy to replace one clip with another.

Time Stretch lets you speed up or slow down the speed of the video for things like creating a slow motion effect in your movie. You can also click the Reverse Speed checkbox to have your video go backward (figure 4.4).

When using the Time Stretch feature make sure you apply it to the clip before placing it on the timeline otherwise the new settings will not be applied to your video. If you make changes after adding the clip to the timeline you will have to remove it and re-add it again with the new changes to have them apply to the video.

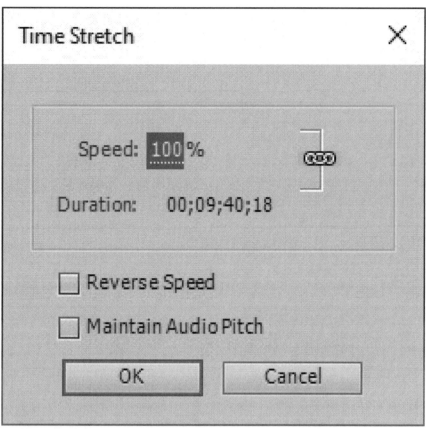

Figure 4.4

Open Clip in Monitor will open the particular video clip in a separate player window allowing you to view it outside of your timeline.

Edit Original will open the clip in your default movie player program.

Run Auto Analyzer will take your clip and break it down into a bunch of smaller clips that Premiere chooses based on things such as scenes containing faces or scenes that might be fuzzy or out of focus allowing you to either use or remove that part of the clip (figure 4.5).

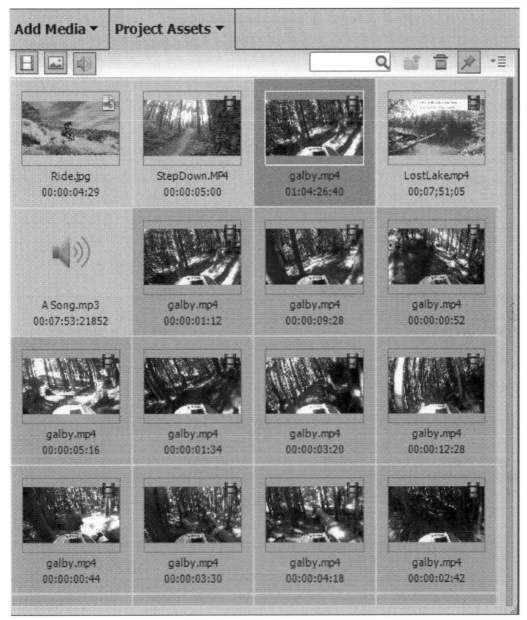

Figure 4.5

At the top of the Project Assets section (figure 4.6), you will find some additional options to manage your media. At the top left, there is a section with three buttons that you can use to hide either video, photos or music from your assets. There is also a search box you can use in case you have so many assets that they are hard to keep track of.

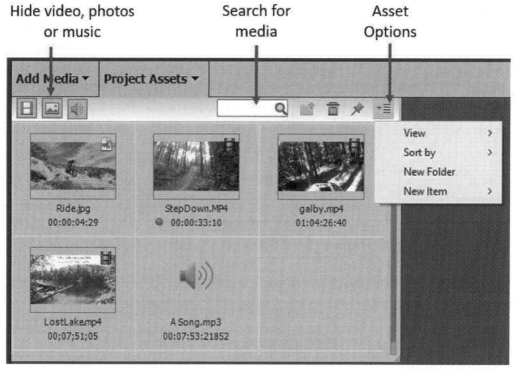

Figure 4.6

The asset options section at the top right has some other things you can do such as change the view of your assets as well as sort them by name, duration or date. The *New Item* section allows you to create things such as Titles, black screens and adjustment layers on the spot.

Cropping Video Footage

When it comes to using the footage that you have recorded with your camera, it will be a rare occurrence that you actually use every minute of your footage. Most of the time you will be doing things like editing out the beginning or ending of your video and also some moments in-between.

In order to remove certain parts of your footage, you will need to crop them out and delete the sections you don't want to be in your final movie. This is a very easy process to do as long as you are careful and don't delete the footage you meant to keep. To complete this task you will need to have your video placed in your timeline since that is where the cropping process will be done from.

Figure 4.7 shows my timeline with a video clip (LostLake.mp4) as well as a song clip (A Song.mp3) place on the timeline. My goal is to remove the first part of the video since I don't want my final movie to start from the start of my actual footage. What I like to do is play the video and watch it on the preview screen and then pause it where I want to make my crop. If you know the approximate area that you want to crop you can drag the playback location marker to where you think you will want to crop your video and then play it back from there until you find the right spot.

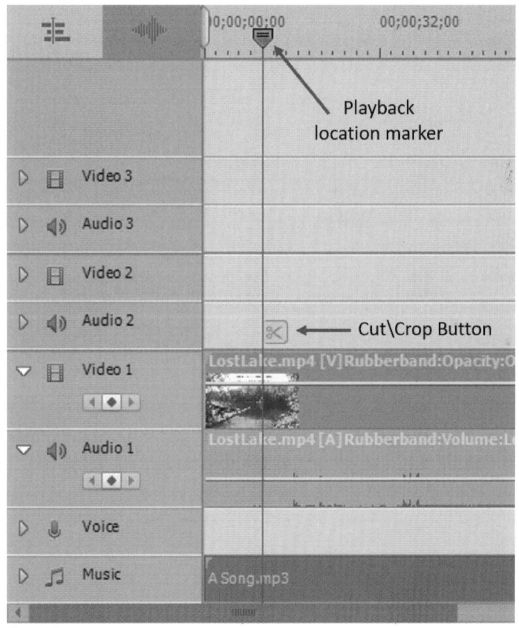

Figure 4.7

The most important thing to remember when it comes to cropping is to make sure that you have the right clip highlighted. In figure 4.7 I have two clips so if I meant to crop the video footage but have the music clip highlighted then it will be the music clip that gets cropped. So once I have the appropriate clip selected and have the playback location marker in the right spot, all I need to do is click the cut\crop scissors icon to have Premiere split the clip at that exact spot as seen in figure 4.8. I moved the playback location marker out of the way to make it easier to see the split in the clip.

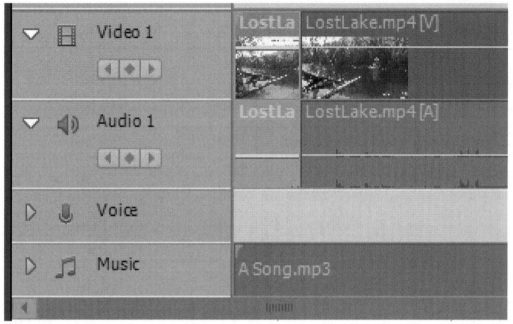

Figure 4.8

Now I can simply click on the left clip since that is the part that I want to remove and press the delete key on my keyboard or right click that clip and choose *Delete*. Figure 4.9 shows what happens if I make two cuts in the middle of a clip to crop out a section that is not at the beginning or end of the video.

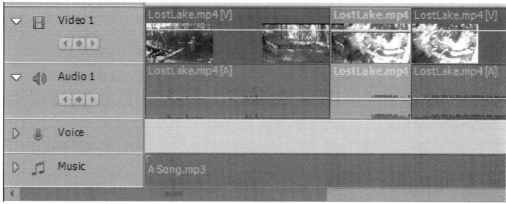

Figure 4.9

When You delete a part of the video, Premiere SHOULD remove the space and connect the two parts of the clips together but sometimes I find that it leaves them separated as you can see in figure 4.10.

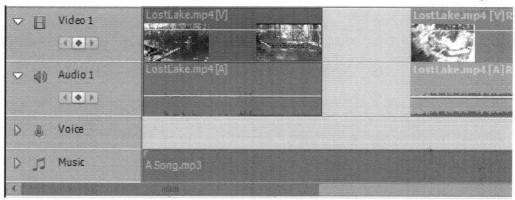

Figure 4.9

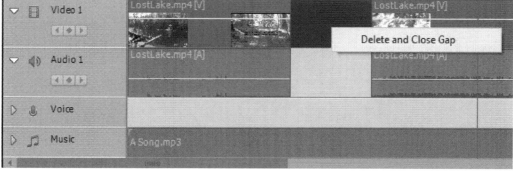

Figure 4.10

When this happens you can either drag the clip on the right over to connect it to the left clip, click in-between both clips and press the delete key on your keyboard or right click in-between the clips and choose *Delete and Close Gap*.

Be careful when dragging separate clips to "connect" them back together. It's easy to drag too far and overlap the clips which will automatically crop the one on the left by the amount that you overlapped it with the clip from the right. Premiere won't tell you that it's doing this extra cropping so you might not even realize it happened until it's too late.

Once you close the gap between clips then the transition between them will be seamless and you won't see any pause or break in the video when it goes from one part of the clip to the next.

Adding a Static Image File

Just because your final video is going to be a video doesn't mean that you can't have any still photos in your movie to help highlight certain aspects of your film. For example, you might want to have a picture of the cruise ship show on the screen for a certain amount of time before the video of your vacation cruise begins. Or you might find yourself wanting to have a picture show on top of your video like your company logo in the corner of the movie.

Adding a static image is just as easy as adding a video and all you need to do is first get your picture into your project assets like you would your video files. Figure 4.11 shows that I added a smiley face picture to my assets which I will be using in a bit. Also notice that I have the picture called **Ride.jpg** already in my project assets.

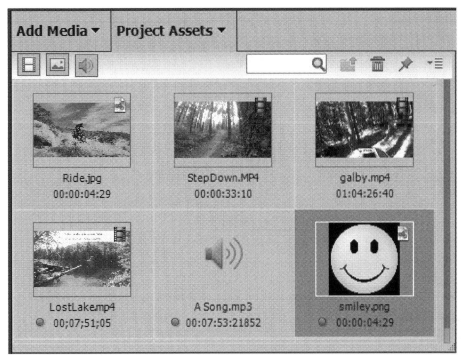

Figure 4.11

First I am going to show you how to add a still image that will display on the screen for as long as you set it to. For the start of my video, I want to have a still image of a mountain biker showing on the screen while my music starts playing. There are two ways I can go about this to get the exact same results. I can either put my image file in front of my video so it will play first and then move on to playing the video as shown in figure 4.12.

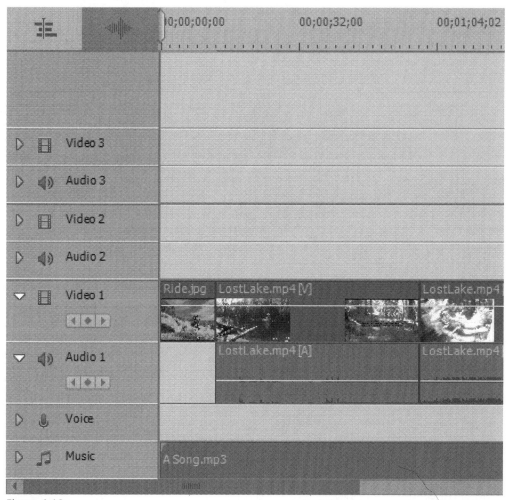

Figure 4.12

Or I can add my image to its own track on the timeline (Video 2) and position it so it doesn't overlap the video file that is on Video 1 (figure 4.13). This way it will show the image file first since its more to the left that the video is on the timeline.

Figure 4.13

If I were to have them overlapping then it would play both at the same time as you can see in figure 4.14. How much they would overlap would be determined by the size of the photo in relation to the size of the video. I shrunk down the size of the photo a bit to better illustrate the overlapping effect.

Figure 4.14

When you add a picture to your video you will need to make sure that it matches the sizing of your project otherwise you will end up with it being too small as shown in figure 4.15 or having it be too large for your video as shown in figure 4.16.

Figure 4.15

Figure 4.16

Fortunately, when you add a photo you have the option drag to resize it to fit the window size of your project. If you look closely at figure 4.15 you will see the dots at the sides and corners of the image. You can click and hold on those to resize the picture so it fits within the black box and that way it will be the same size as your video footage when it comes time to play it back.

Another common usage for images within a video is to have them overlay on top of the footage when using something like a company logo or website address.

Going back to the smiley face image that I added to my project assets, now I want to add that to my video, and have it show at the bottom right corner of my video throughout the whole movie.

To do this I simply drag the smiley face image to my timeline and Premiere adds it to the video preview screen. But as you can see in figure 4.17, the image is way too big and also not where I want it to be, but this is a simple fix. All I need to do is resize the image using the dots on the corner of the image when I click on it and then drag it where I would like it to be on the screen. The results are shown in figure 4.18

Figure 4.17

Figure 4.18

To make the smiley face show during the entire movie I will need to click on the smiley face clip in the timeline and drag it to extend it so it takes up the length of the entire video otherwise it will stop displaying when it gets to the end of that clip.

Adding Text

One thing many people like to do with their movies is add text to be used for things such as a title or to describe something such as the location of the footage the viewer is watching. There are several ways to add text in Premiere and fortunately the process for doing each one is pretty similar.

The most basic way to add text is to use the basic text method or as Premiere calls it, Default Text. What this does is just add a simple line of text into your video that you can then format the way you like. You can do this by going to the *Text* menu item and then choosing *Default Text*.

Figure 4.19 shows what happens when you choose the Default Text option. As you can see, it simply adds some text that says ADD TEXT to the middle of the screen and it's up to you to format this text to make it appear the way you like.

Figure 4.19

As you can see in figure 4.20, Premiere also adds the text clip to your timeline in an available video "slot". In my project, the text clip is named Title 01.

If you want to see the thumbnail view of your video, image, text or audio clip then you can simply click on the right pointing arrow at the left of the clip on the timeline to make it point downwards. This comes in handy when editing your movie because it makes it easier to see what clips you are actually working on.

Figure 4.20

Before getting into how to format your text I want to show you the other kinds of text you can insert into your project. If you choose the *Default Roll* option then Premiere will create a scrolling text "roll" that will scroll up the screen with the text that you add as seen in figure 4.21.

Figure 4.21

Finally, we have the *Default Crawl* choice which will give you a main title on top and then text underneath and they will both scroll from right to left across the screen as seen in figure 4.22.

Figure 4.22

No matter what text option you choose, you will have most of the same options for formatting your text, but you may find a few differences between the way they can be altered.

To format the text type that you are using within your video simply double click the text clip on the timeline to bring up the text adjustments pane. From there you will have several tabs that each offer different types of formatting options. Figure 4.23 shows the *Text* tab where you can change things such as the font\typestyle, font size and color as well as alignment and justification settings. The green T tools In the *Mode* section are for editing text and the arrow tool is used for moving your text around.

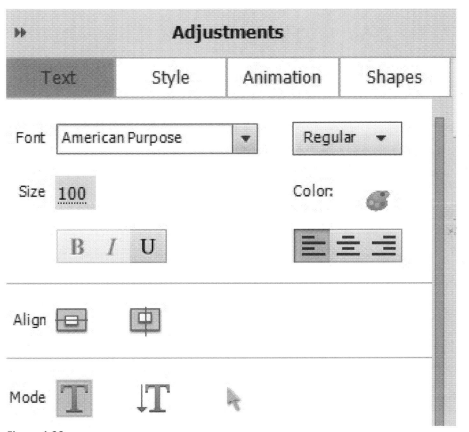

Figure 4.23

Figure 4.24 shows the *Style* tab which is used to apply custom built in styles to your text. These styles add elements such as outlines and shadows to your text.

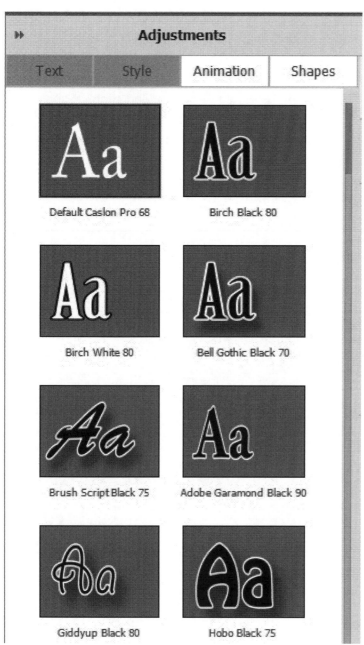

Figure 4.24

Figure 4.25 shows the *Animation* tab that can be used to apply a custom animation or motion effect to your text such as have each letter appear one at a time from the bottom of the screen. Clicking on the play button on one of the animations will show you a preview of how it will look if you were to use it. If you want to apply it to your text all you need to do is double click on it. Then you can go to your timeline and playback the video and see how it looks in the preview screen.

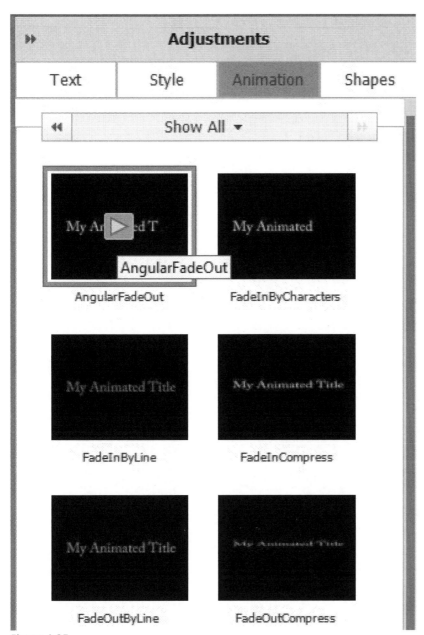

Figure 4.25

Finally, we have the *Shapes* tab (figure 4.26) which is where you can add shapes to your videos such as boxes, circles and lines. Then you can do things such as change their color and opacity (make them see through). Figure 4.27 shows an example of a roundish shape I place over my Lost Lake text and then make opaque so it would be see through. I also applied a style to my text to make it stand out a little more.

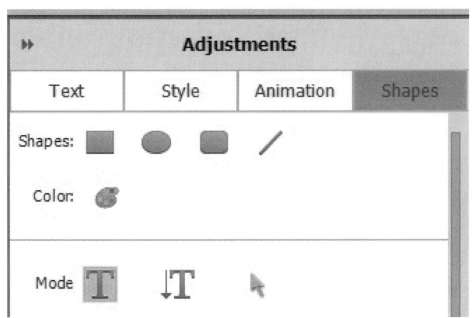

Figure 4.26

Figure 4.27

Motion Title

Another type of text effect you can add to your movies is a Motion Title. These are custom pre-formatted animated graphics that you can apply to your movie and then edit so the text says whatever you would like it to say. You can add a Motion Title from the Text menu just like we did for the other text objects.

Figure 4.28 shows an example of one of the built in Motion Titles and it includes the background image as well, but the background, text and graphic can all be edited in case you want to customize it to better suit your video.

Figure 4.28

Once you apply a Motion Title to your project you can double click it to make your adjustments just like we did when we added the text but the choices you have will be a little different for the Motion Title. There are three main areas where you can make changes from.

The *Text* adjustments allow you to do the same type of text formatting we did before and you can change things such as the font as well as its size and color. You can also apply custom styles and animations to the text.

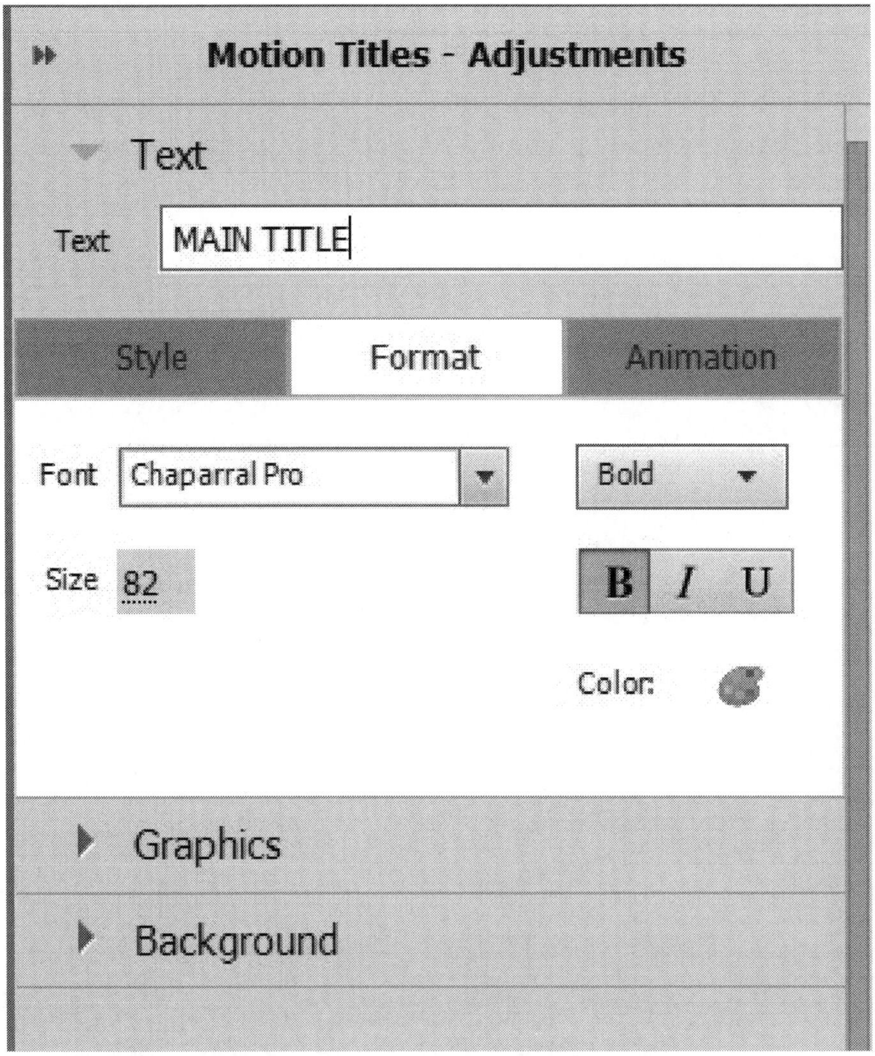

Figure 4.29

The *Graphics* adjustments allow you to change the ribbon style and color if you don't like the default look. Once you pick a new style simply click on the Apply button to have it applied to your project (figure 4.30).

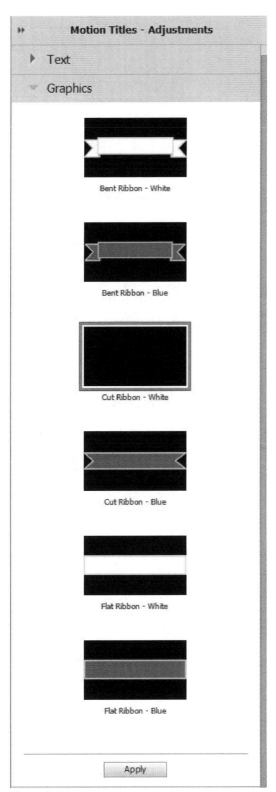

Figure 4.30

The Background adjustment is something you will most likely want to play around with since you will most likely not want to use the background images that come included with the Motion Titles. There are four ways to customize the background image and I will now go over each one so you have an idea of what they do.

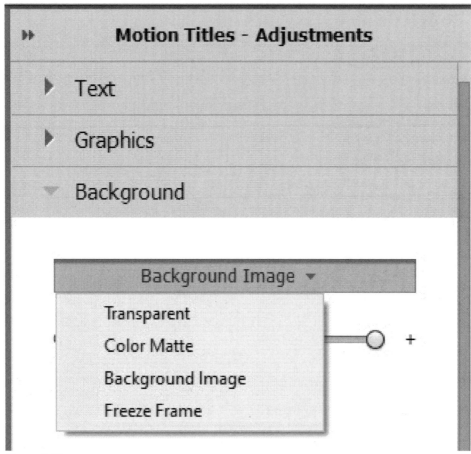

Figure 4.31

Transparent
This will hide the background image that comes with the Motion Title and show your video as the background as shown in figure 4.32.

Figure 4.32

Color Matte
Using this option you can apply a solid colored background to your Motion Title, and you can choose any color you like.

Figure 4.33

Background Image
This will apply the default background picture that comes with the Motion Title as shown back in figure 4.28. You can set the opacity level if you would like the picture to be semi-transparent.

Freeze Frame
By default, Premiere will choose a frame from your video as a background image when you apply the Motion Title. But if you want to choose a different frame you can drag the Motion Title clip in the timeline to a new frame of your choosing and then click on the *Refresh Frame* button to have that new frame be the background of your Motion Title.

Adding a Music File
Many people like to have music playing in the background of their videos to liven them up and keep people interested in watching them. With Premiere it's very easy to add either your own music to your video or use one of the built in songs that come with the software.

You add music to your project just like you would a video clip by adding the media to your project assets and then add it to your timeline at the appropriate spot in your project. You should already know how to add media to your project assets and also how to add a clip to your timeline by now so now I will show you how to use one of the built in audio clips.

To get to these audio clips you will need to click on the music note icon (figure 4.34) and choose one of the songs from the various categories. You can click on each one to hear a sample before deciding if you want to add it to your project or not.

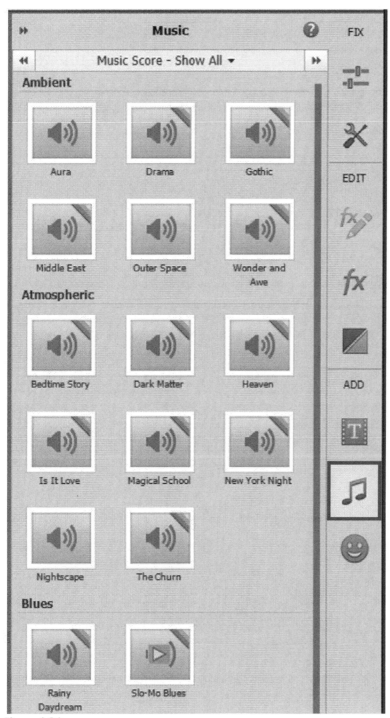

Figure 4.34

When you find the song you like, simply drag it to a Music track slot on the timeline and when you release the mouse you will be asked to choose an intensity level and whether or not you want the audio clip to be made to fit the entire timeline.

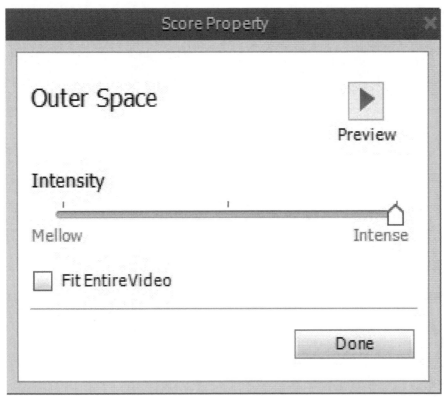

Figure 4.35

I can't really tell the difference between mellow and intense when it comes to the intensity level but it most likely will be more noticeable based on what song you choose.

If you want the song to fit the entire length of the movie from start to finish then make sure when you drag the song into the timeline that you release it at the very left or beginning of your video otherwise it will only fill your timeline from the point where you placed it on the timeline to the end of the video. Then you will have to drag to the left to expand it to fit the entire timeline.

Figure 4.36 shows my project after adding the sound and you can see it at the bottom of the timeline. I also wanted to illustrate how things are starting to look a little crowded in my Project Assets window after adding all of these elements to my project.

Figure 4.36

Adjusting Volume Levels

Now that I have all of these video and audio (music) clips in my project I should take a moment to check and adjust the volume levels of my clips as needed. When you have multiple video clips that play one after the other you might find that the volume levels are not the same between clips and you don't want your volume jumping around from loud to quiet throughout your movie.

There are a couple of ways to adjust the volume levels of your clips if needed. One way is to highlight the video or audio clip you want to adjust the level on and then click on the first icon under the *FIX* section on the Adjustments toolbar as shown in figure 4.37. Then go down to *Volume* and adjust the volume level higher or lower as needed.

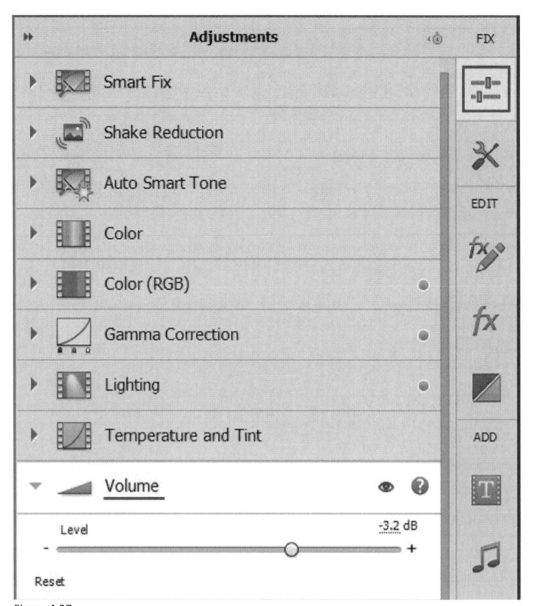

Figure 4.37

Another way to increase or decrease volume on a clip is to drag the volume level line up or down to adjust the clip volume. All you need to do is hold your mouse over the volume level line until it makes a double arrow and then either drag up to increase the volume or drag down to decrease the volume. As you are dragging, Premiere will tell you what your volume level is based on where the line is on the clip.

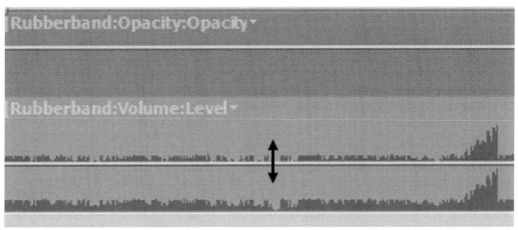

Figure 4.38

I always like to play back the video to check the volume levels for the entire clip and see if I need to make any further adjustments.

Chapter 5 – Enhancing Your Videos

Now that you have the basics down when it comes to getting your media into Premiere and editing that media so you have only the video and audio that you want to use in your movie, it's now time to add a little pizzazz to your video to give it that professional touch.

Premiere comes with many built in effects and transitions that are super easy to apply to your video but will make it look like you spent hours working on your movie. There are also many tools you can use to fine tune the way your overall video looks by making simple changes to colors and lighting or by creating custom menus for DVD chapters.

In this chapter, I will be going over most of these tools and effects so you will have a good idea of what you can do to customize your footage and how to go about doing it. Some of these features I have already gone over in earlier chapters but for the most part, this will be all new material.

The tools and effects etc. that I will be going over in this chapter can be found on the toolbar to the right of the workspace as seen in figure 5.1. I mentioned this toolbar back in Chapter 2 so it should look familiar. The toolbar is broken down into three categories which are Fix, Edit and Add and I will be going over the choices in each one of these categories next.

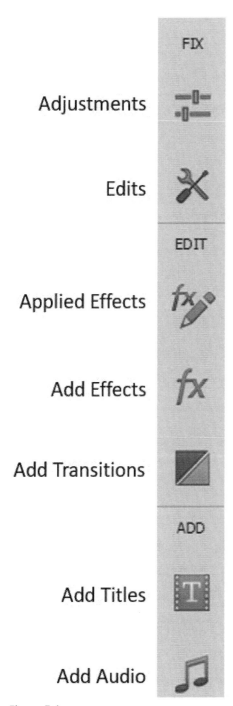

Figure 5.1

Adjustments

Under the *Fix* category (figure 5.2) we have a whole bunch of options\adjustments that we can use to adjust various aspects of our video and audio. Some of them should be obvious but others may not.

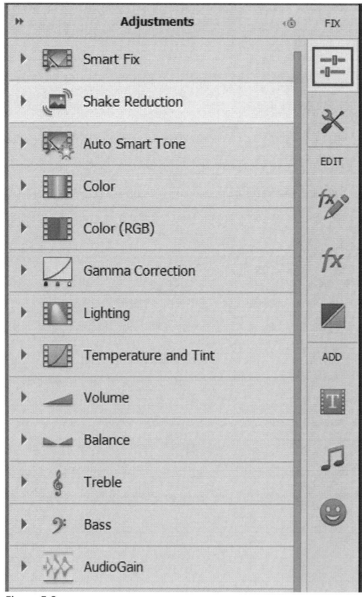

Figure 5.2

I will now go over all of the adjustments from the Fix category to give you a better idea of what each one of them does. There will be many adjustments here that you will probably never use so don't think you need to be an expert at all of them. Also, keep in mind that just because these adjustments are under the Fix category doesn't mean they will always make your video look better or your audio sound better.

Smart Fix – You can use this adjustment to have Premiere analyze your video and then automatically apply adjustments based on what it sees in your footage. If you do use this you should watch the entire clip afterward to make sure it didn't actually make anything look worse rather than better.

Shake Reduction – If your footage came out shaky for some reason such as you were using an action camera like a GoPro on some rough terrain then you can try to see if the Shake Reduction feature can smooth it out. In my experience, it doesn't work too well but you might have better results based on your footage.

Auto Smart Tone – This will change the visual tones of your footage based on what Premiere sees and think needs to be adjusted to make your video look better. There is a *Custom* button you can click which will allow you to decide what types of adjustments look better. When you click on Custom you get several choices shown to you (one at each corner) and you can then drag the center arrows towards the corner that looks better to you and Premiere will adjust the tone as you drag until things look the way you want them to (figure 5.3).

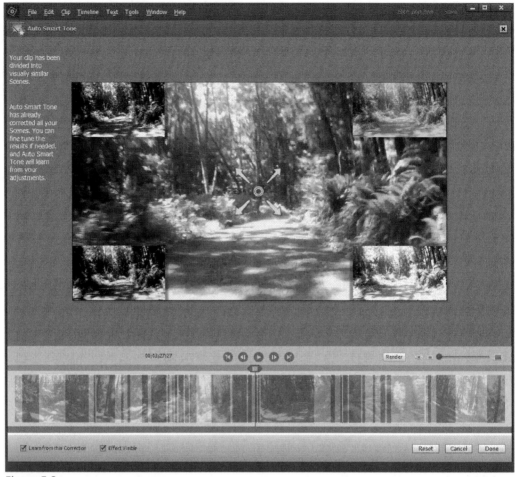

Figure 5.3

Color – From the color adjustment section you can change color attributes based on the hue, lightness, saturation and vibrance attributes of your video. There are many built in suggestions that you can click on to have applied or you can use the sliders as shown in figure 5.4 to change the color composition of your video. If you don't like what you see after playing with the sliders simply click on *Reset* at the bottom of the section.

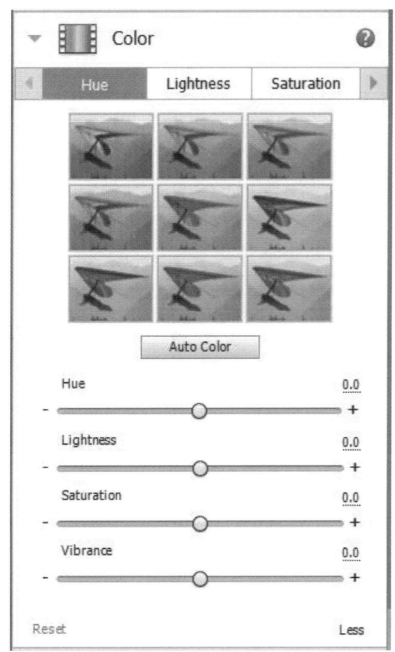

Figure 5.4

Color (RGB) – This is similar to the other Color setting except you are making changes to the individual red, green and blue aspects of the color spectrum which allows for a completely different type of color adjustment. It works the same way with the preset choices as well as the individual sliders that you can use to make your changes.

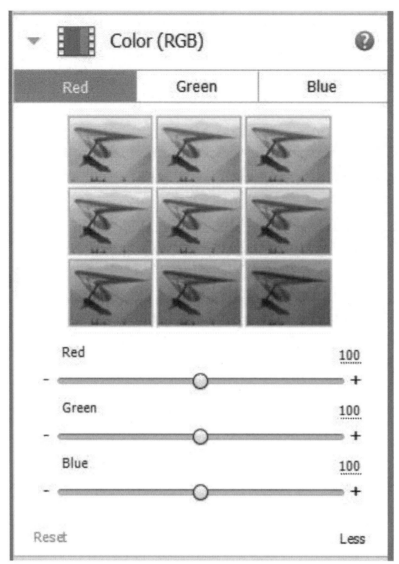

Figure 5.5

Gamma Correction – Gamma correction is a way to change lighting features without dramatically changing the shadows and highlights. Once again there are some built in options to choose from as well as a slider where you can manually adjust the gamma levels.

Lighting – The Lighting section is one of those adjustments areas that you will probably find yourself using more than some of the others. Here you can adjust common lighting settings such as brightness, contrast, exposure as well as black and white levels. Once again there are built in choices or you can use the slider bars. There are also *Auto Levels* and *Auto Contrast* buttons that you can take your chances with. If you want to have Premiere do its own thing you can check the *Auto Fix* box and see how it looks to you.

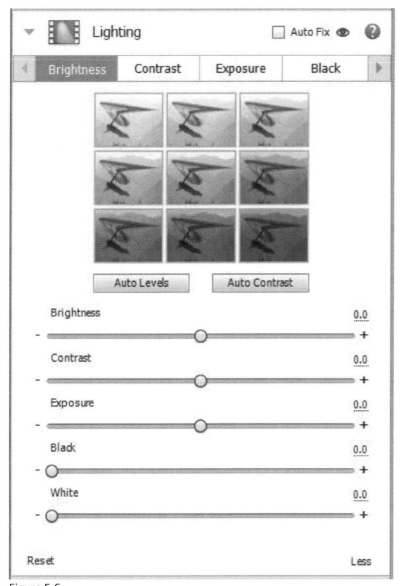

Figure 5.6

The eyeball icon at the top right of these adjustment tools allows you to toggle the changes on or off so you can see how your footage looks with the changes applied and without. It gives you an easy way to determine if the adjustments really made things look better or not.

Temperature and Tint – These adjustments will change the overall coloring as to how warm your footage looks (temperature) and also allows you to change the coloring as if you were looking through various types of sunglasses (tint).

Volume – I discussed changing volume in the last chapter and it's pretty self-explanatory how this feature works.

Balance – This controls the audio levels between the left and right channels (speakers) in case you want one side to be louder than the other.

Treble – This controls the amount of treble in your sound which is the higher frequencies of the sound spectrum.

Bass – This controls the amount of bass in your sound which is the lower\deeper frequencies of the sound spectrum.

AudioGain – This is similar to volume but differs because it applies to the levels applied to the sound input while volume applies to the sound output but for practical purposes you can think of gain as another way to adjust the volume levels in your project.

When applying positive or negative gain you can enter the number you want to increase the gain by or enter a negative number (-15 for example) to decrease the gain. Once you enter your numeric value, click on the *OK* button to apply it to that clip. I like to use increments of 5 or 10 and then play back the video and see if I need to make any adjustments.

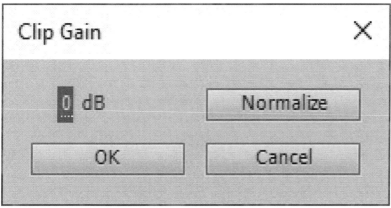

Figure 5.7

You can also click the *Normalize* button to have Premiere automatically increase the gain where it's too quiet or reduce the gain where it's too loud. If you do choose this option you might want to review that entire clip to make sure that Premiere didn't increase or decrease the gain too much.

If it isn't obvious, to apply one of these adjustments to a clip you need to have that clip highlighted on the timeline first otherwise it won't be applied, and you won't be able to see any previews while making the adjustments.

Tools

Next on the list are the various Tools that can be used to perform a variety of tasks such as capturing screenshots and creating slow motion scenes from your video. I will now go over each of the items from the tools Video and Audio sections.

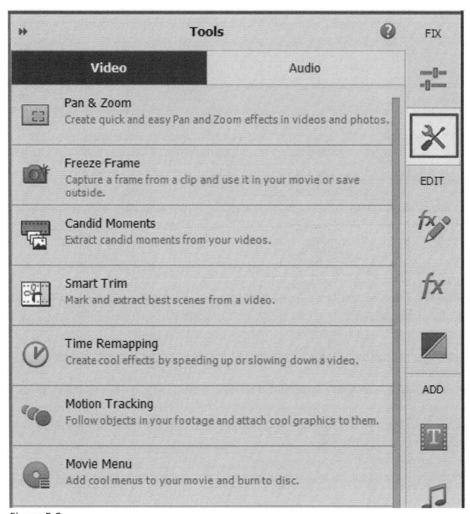

Figure 5.8

Video Tools

Since I obviously can't show you examples of any motion based video tools I will do my best to explain what they do.

Pan & Zoom – If you want to have a part of your movie have a custom section where it zooms in to a particular spot or pans to or from a particular spot then you can use the Pan & Zoom feature. This can be used on video clips, but I find it works better on still images since they are not in motion while you are trying to zoom into it. I suppose if your video clip was a still shot this would work the same.

Figure 5.9 shows a still image that I have in my timeline and it might be hard to see but there is a box around the outer edge with the number 1 in the lower left corner. Then there is a smaller box around the biker with the number 2 in the lower left corner which I made bigger for you to see in figure 5.10. The first box is the initial zoom level while the second box highlights where the frame will be zoomed into.

Figure 5.9

In figure 5.10 you can see the area that will be shown for the final zoom and also see that the shot will pan to the lower right for 5 seconds because of the arrow in the middle of the box. You can drag this box around your screen to tell Premiere which direction you want the camera to pan and where you want it to zoom into. This will take a little playing with on your part to get the hang of it. Just remember that you can click the *Preview* button to see how it will look before clicking on *Done* to have it applied to your clip.

You can also add multiple frames using this tool and have the camera zoom and pan all over the place if you really want to get wild with it!

Figure 5.10

Freeze Frame – While working with your video you might come across a scene that would make a good still photo for your movie or even make a good photo that you can use for other purposes. If this is the case all you need to do is pause the video on that section and click on Freeze Frame.

After clicking on Freeze Frame, Premiere will open up that frame in a new window and you will have several choices as to what to do with it (figure 5.11). The Extract Candid Moments will option will be discussed next, but you can also export it as an image file to your computer or as an image file to your Project Assets that you can then use within your movie (Insert in Movie button).

Figure 5.11

Candid Moments – This tool will analyze your clip and then try to find the best images it can based on what it finds. Then you can use these images for things as making a slide show, using them in your project or just saving them to a folder on your computer.

You can have Premiere exact all the moments it finds by clicking the *Auto Extract* button as seen in figure 5.12 or you can move the slider over each picture you want and click the camera button to have that particular image added to your extracted moments. Then you can export them to a folder, slide show or your timeline from there.

Figure 5.12

Smart Trim – This feature is rather interesting because it will analyze a clip and then mark what it thinks are the best scenes from that clip. It will base its analysis on either people, action or a mix of the two based on what you select as seen in figure 5.13. There is also a slider to have it use more or less of your footage in the trim process depending on if you would like the final scene to be longer or shorter.

Once it does its thing, it will show you the scenes it has selected at the bottom of the screen. From there you can preview the selected scenes as one shot, and it will apply transitions between the scenes automatically as long as the *Apply Transitions* checkbox is checked.

If you don't like one of the scenes it has selected then you can click the X at the top right corner of that scene to remove it and you can also drag to stretch out the selected scenes to make them longer if desired.

116

Figure 5.13

If there is some footage that has not been automatically selected and you would like to add it to the scene selections then all you need to do is place the marker on that scene and click the *Mark Manually* button.

Once you approve of all the selected scenes then you can export them to your timeline as one clip by clicking on *Export Merged* or you can have each scene be its own clip on the timeline by clicking on *Export Individual*.

When you go back to your timeline you will see that your clip has been shortened since it now only contains the trimmed scenes that you selected.

Before

Figure 5.14

After

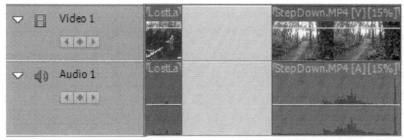

Figure 5.15

Time Remapping – This tool gives you the ability to speed up or slow down the timing of your footage and also allows you to make clips play backward if desired. The way it works is you click on an area that you want to change and then click on the *Add Time Zone* button which will bring up the speed changing options (figure 5.16) where you can choose your speed and also if you want to reverse your clip. You can drag the slider to apply the time change to more or less of your footage. If you select the *Frame Blending* button then Premiere will try and smooth out your motion changes for you.

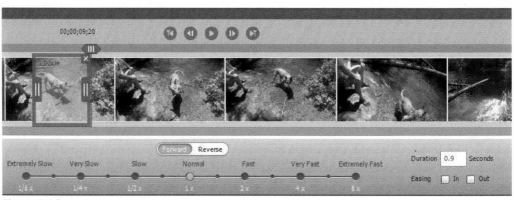

Figure 5.16

One thing to keep in mind when slowing down or speeding up video is that the related audio might go out of sync. If you don't need the audio to be there or are planning to use a music clip over your video then you can have Premiere remove the audio from the remapped video when it asks.

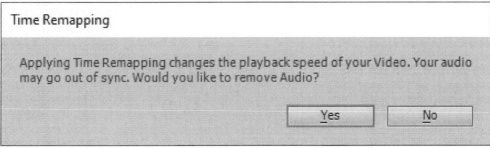

Time Remapping

Applying Time Remapping changes the playback speed of your Video. Your audio may go out of sync. Would you like to remove Audio?

Yes   No

Figure 5.17

Then you will be taken back to your timeline and the sections that you chose to have remapped will be in place with the new speeds applied.

If you change your mind and want the changes you made to the speed of your clip to be set back to normal then you can simply go back into the Time Remapping tool and remove the remapped sections by clicking on the X at the top right corner of the marked areas of the clip.

Motion Tracking – Motion Tracking is a neat feature that allows you to insert graphics into your video that will follow a moving object as the video goes along. Once you select the clip you want to use this on you will first need to select the object that you want to track. In my case, I drew a box around the dog in figure 5.18 and clicked on *Track Object* since that is what I want to track.

Figure 5.18

Premiere will then analyze the clip and track the movement of the dog so it can be used with the next step.

Next, I will choose the type of graphic I want to have follow the dog in the video. There are several categories to choose from, but I will select a speech bubble for my clip.

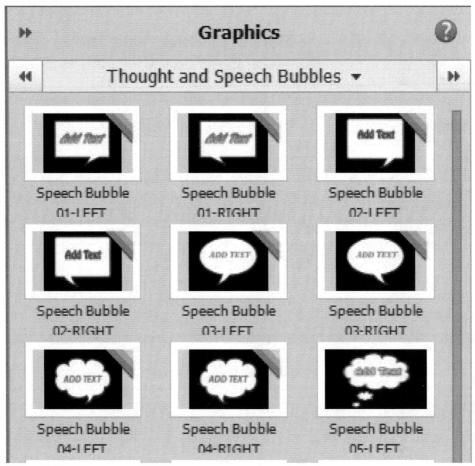

Figure 5.19

Then I will add some custom text to the speech bubble. Now when I play back the video, the speech bubble will follow the dog where it goes throughout the clip (figure 5.20).

Figure 5.20

Movie Menu – If you plan on creating DVD\Blu Ray movies with Premiere then it's possible to add custom menus with scene selection buttons to your final video. The first thing you will need to do is choose one of the menu themes from the various categories that Premiere provides. I will choose the Travel category and then the Road Trip menu as seen in figure 5.21.

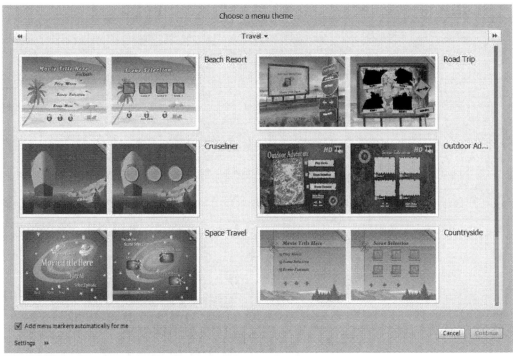

Figure 5.21

Figures 5.22 and 5.23 show the blank main menu and scene selection menu that comes with the Road Trip theme.

Figure 5.22

Figure 5.23

To edit the menu items simply click on the section you want to edit and make your changes. Figure 5.24 and 5.25 show the adjustments I can apply for the main menu title and image.

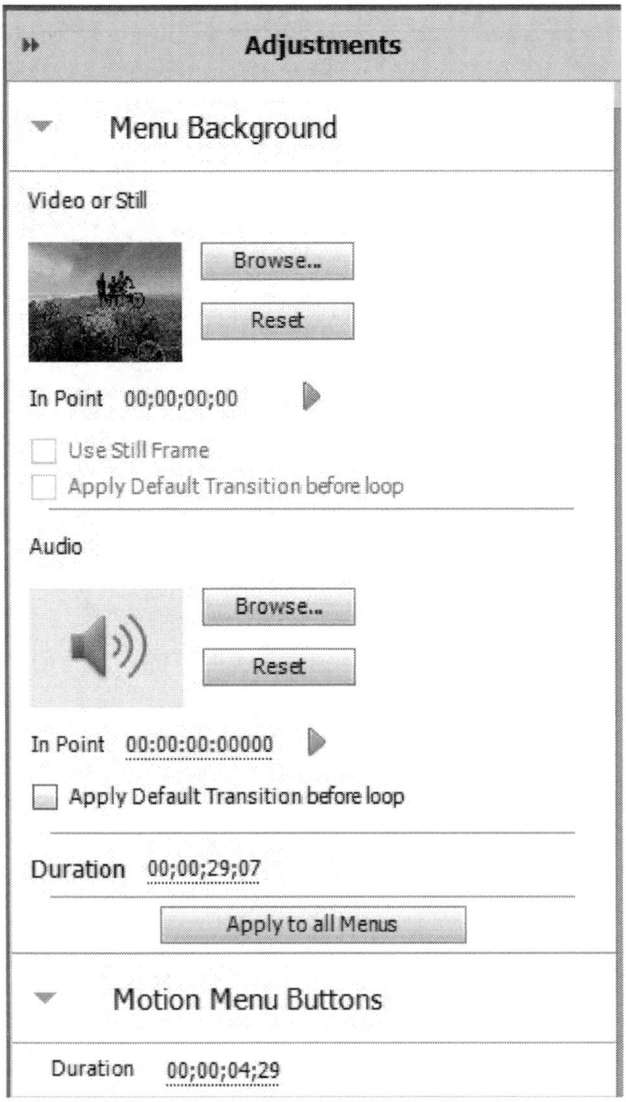

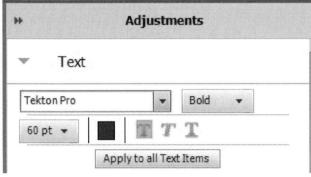

Adjustments

▼ Menu Background

Video or Still

Browse...

Reset

In Point   00;00;00;00   ▶

☐ Use Still Frame
☐ Apply Default Transition before loop

Audio

Browse...

Reset

In Point   00:00:00:00000   ▶

☐ Apply Default Transition before loop

Duration   00;00;29;07

Apply to all Menus

▼ Motion Menu Buttons

Duration   00;00;04;29

Figure 5.24

Adjustments

▼ Text

Tekton Pro   ▼   Bold   ▼

60 pt ▼   T *T* T

Apply to all Text Items

Figure 5.25

124

You can use either a still shot from your video as a menu background image or an actual image file that you have on your computer. If you choose a still shot from your video then you can press the green play button to have the video play and then pause it at the spot you want to use for your background image. The *Motion Menu Buttons* option will let you make a button that runs a short clip from your video.

For the text, you can do things like change the font as well as its color and size. If you want to keep that font appearance consistent with the rest of your menus items you can click on the *Apply to all Text* Items button.

Figure 5.26 shows the results after I added a still image for the menu background and then edited my type to my liking.

Figure 5.26

You can edit the scene menu the same way as the main menu but what differs is how you add the scenes to the scene menu. Scenes are also known as chapters by the way in case that is a term you are used to hearing. The template I used came with two scene spots, but I wanted to add another one so how I did this was to choose a location on my timeline with the marker and then went to the *Markers* menu and chose *Menu Marker > Set Menu Marker* (figure 5.27). You can also right click on the timeline marker and choose Set Menu Marker.

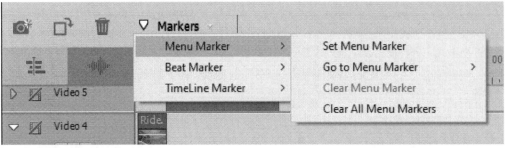

Figure 5.27

One other marker type I want to mention is the *Stop Marker*. These are used to stop the video playback after a scene (chapter) is done playing and then take you back to the main menu. You can insert these at the end of the scene wherever you want to use them. To add a Stop Marker, place the main playback marker where you would want it to be and then go through the same process you did before to add a Menu Marker but instead choose Stop Marker from the Marker Type dropdown menu.

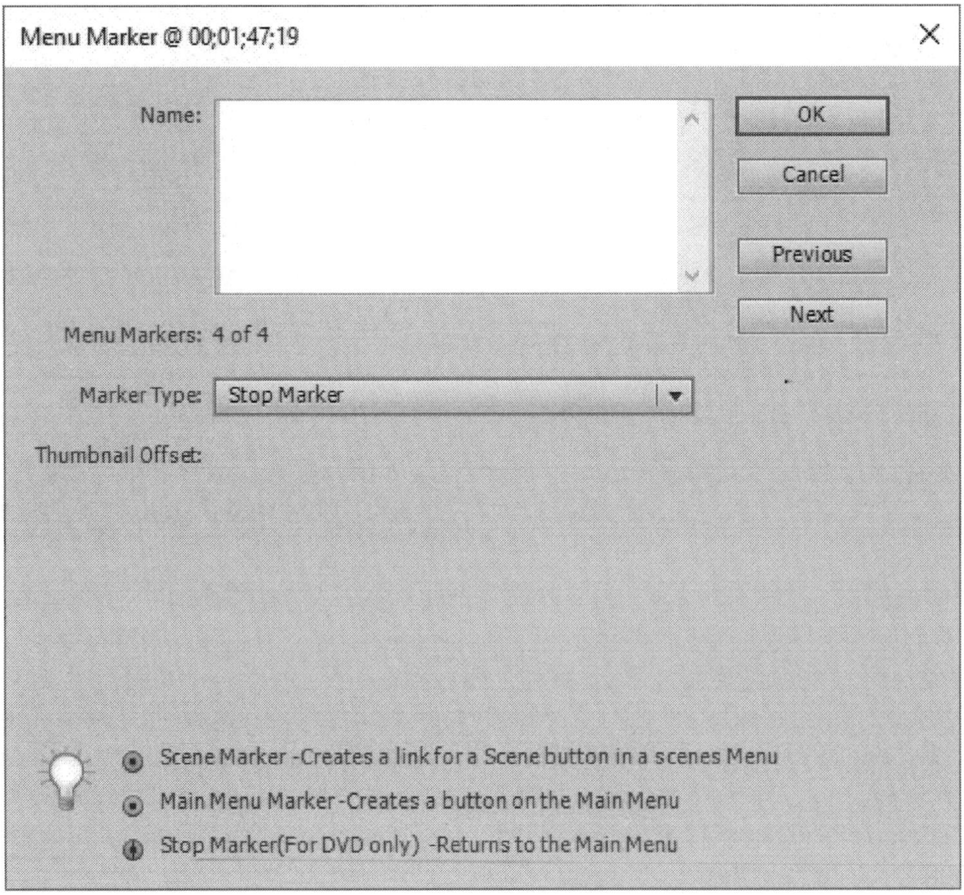

Menu Marker @ 00;01;47;19   ✕

Name: [   ]   [OK]

[Cancel]

[Previous]

[Next]

Menu Markers: 4 of 4

Marker Type: [Stop Marker   ▼]

Thumbnail Offset:

💡 ⦿ Scene Marker -Creates a link for a Scene button in a scenes Menu
    ⦿ Main Menu Marker -Creates a button on the Main Menu
    ⦿ Stop Marker(For DVD only) -Returns to the Main Menu

Figure 5.28

You don't need to worry about adding a name for Stop Markers since they will not be displayed on your main menu.

Figure 5.29 shows the final scene menu that I will be using with my DVD\Blu Ray movie.

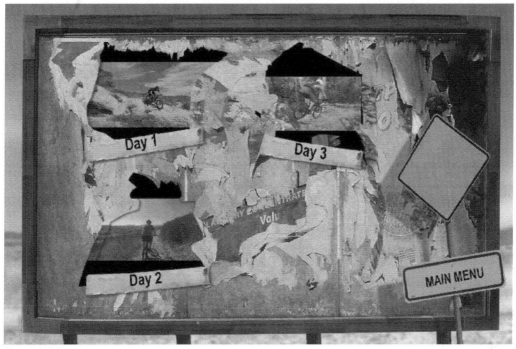

Figure 5.29

When you are finished you can click on the *Preview* button to see how it will all look when you create your final DVD or Blu Ray disk and if things look good then you can click on the *Done* button.

You will then be taken back to your timeline you will see small green circles at the top that indicate all of your chapters or scenes that you created for your movie.

Figure 5.30

Audio Tools

There are not as many audio tools as there are video tools and in fact, there are only three of them which I will now go over.

Figure 5.31

Audio Mixer – This tool can be used to adjust the volume and balance levels in your clips for general sounds, voice and music. It's not like a typical mixer where you can adjust levels for various audio channels to fine tune your sound. As you can see in figure 5.32 there are three parts to the mixer labeled Audio 1, Voice and Music. Each pair has its own level slider that can be used to adjust the volume up or down as well as its own balance control which allows you to adjust the sound to levels for the left and right speakers.

If the audio for your videos was not recorded in stereo (mono) then adjusting the left and right balance levels most likely won't do any good since its technically all one channel and not separated into different sides. So if you play with the balance knob and it doesn't change anything then that is probably the case.

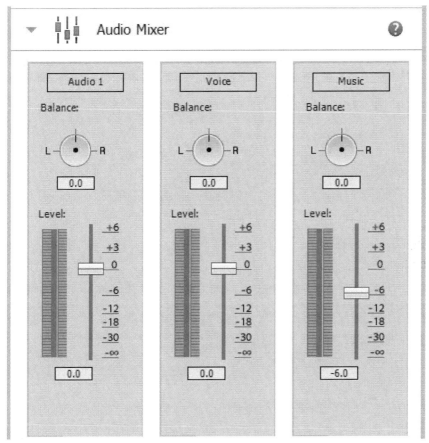

Figure 5.32

When using the Audio Mixer, have the video playing so you can make the adjustment as you are listening to it. You won't see anything changing on your timeline until you pause the video playback. Then you will see the changes on the level on the volume portion of the track that corresponds to the changes you made with the mixer.

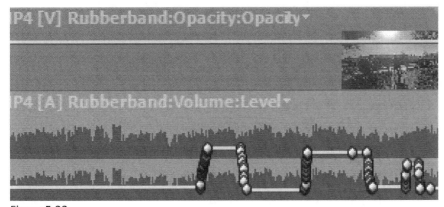

Figure 5.33

Narration – If you have a need to add commentary over the action in your video then you can use the Narration tool to do so. All you need to do is start the video where you want the commentary to begin and press record and speak into your microphone as the video is playing on your screen. When you are finished click on the Stop button and Premiere will place the narration audio on the timeline as a voice clip with the video in the appropriate place as seen in figure 5.35.

Figure 5.34

Figure 5.35

Obviously, you need to have a working microphone connected to your computer to use this feature and you can get one relatively cheap online or at your local electronics store. Most computers will recognize the new microphone when you connect it so there isn't much involved in getting it working on your computer.

If the microphone is not picking up your voice at an appropriate level then you can increase the *Mic Sensitivity* slider and see if it makes a difference in the recording level. If you don't want to hear the audio that is in your video or any other audio like music while recording your narration you can check the box that says *Mute audio while recording* to do so.

Smart Mixer – This tool is designed to give you an overall better volume level for all your tracks when you have multiple audio sources by balancing them according to your specifications. By default, your main video clip is in the foreground, but you might want to have your narration (Voice) have the main focus when it comes to sound levels. Using this tool you can tell Premiere what order you want your audio to be in when it comes to sound priority. Once you have chosen your settings, click the Apply button to have Premiere apply them to your project.

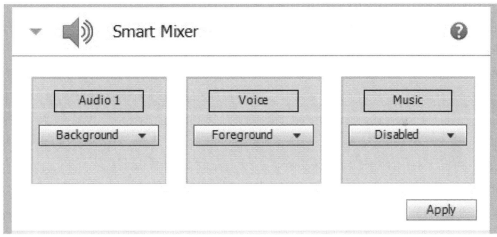

Figure 5.36

How well this works will depend on the tracks you have in your video. I don't find too much use for the Smart Mixer for my videos but that doesn't mean you won't.

Applied Effects

You may run into a situation where you didn't have the best person for the job filming your video and maybe they didn't get close enough to the object they were supposed to be filming or maybe they even were holding the camera upside down!

If that's the case then you can go into the *Applied Effects* settings and do some adjustments to get things looking the way they were supposed to. Within the Applied Effects section, you have two categories, *Motion* and *Opacity*.

The *Motion* settings allow you to do things such as change the scale of the clip kind of like zooming in or out of the video. Figure 5.38 shows the default scale size while figure 5.39 shows what happens when the scale is increased which technically zooms into the video.

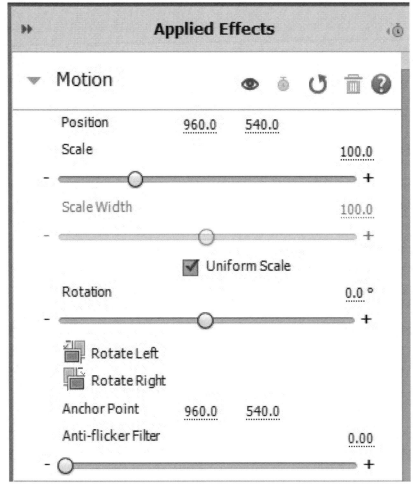

Figure 5.37

When using the Scale feature make sure to have the Uniform Scale box checked otherwise your footage will get "stretched out" as seen in figure 5.40.

Figure 5.38

Figure 5.39

Figure 5.40

If you use the Scale feature, you will find that you might have to re-center the object in your video that you are zooming in on because it might end up off the screen. You can do this by clicking and dragging the video in the preview screen to the position where everything fits the way it is supposed to.

The other main feature of the Motion section is the *Rotation* option which will let you rotate your clip in any direction you like. You can either rotate it freely with your mouse or type in a positive number to spin it to the right or a negative number to spin it to the left. This number represents the degree of rotation.

The *Anchor Point* setting is used to tell Premiere where the clip will be rotated from. Normally it's rotated from the center, but you can change that by entering new values here.

The *Anti Flicker* setting can be used in special situations where you are going to watch your movie on TVs that used interlaced displays. In these situations, you might get some flickering on the screen along the edges of your movie. You can use the Anti Flicker adjustment to try and reduce this effect.

The *Opacity* section can be used to change the overall transparency of your video and can be used to have one clip fade in or fade out to another one or even have two clips overlapping each other and both appearing on the screen at the same time. There is an *Opacity* slider that controls how opaque or transparent the clip will be and then under *Blend Mode,* you can choose from a variety of blending styles such as lighten, darken, dissolve and so on. Figure 5.42 shows an example of two clips blended together.

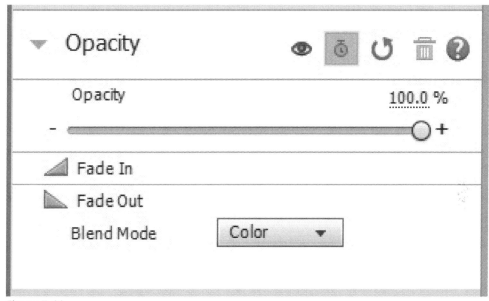

Figure 5.41

Figure 5.42

Keyframes

One important aspect of using the Motion and Opacity tools is learning how to use keyframes to animate these effects otherwise they are not super useful since you most likely won't want an entire clip zoomed in or rotated an odd angle. In most situations, you will want just a section of a clip to zoom in, fade in or rotate etc.

Keyframes are used to signal the start and end points of an animation and need to be manually set in order to be used in your video. Keyframes are an advanced topic and would be difficult to explain in writing so I would recommend finding a video online or on YouTube that demonstrates how to use them if this is something you would eventually like to play with.

As you start using other effects in Premiere you will notice that they will show up under Applied Effects when they have any attributes that can be changed that affect motion etc.

Effects

The main Effects section is where you will most likely find yourself playing around since it's much more straightforward than the Applied Effects I discussed in the last section. Here you will use more of a click and apply method meaning you chose an effect and Premiere will apply it to your clip (except for the Keying effects). The Effects section is broken down into Video and Audio effects and there are some pretty neat built in effects to choose from.

In the Video section, you can see that there are many types of effects categories to choose from and if you were to try and create these types of effects on your own it would take you quite a bit of time to accomplish what you can do in a few clicks from the Effects section.

You have probably figured out by now that you need to select a clip in your timeline before applying any type of change to it, but just in case you haven't been playing along I thought I would point that out. Just make sure you have the clip you want to apply a change to selected before making that change.

Figure 5.43 shows just a portion of the available effects that you have to choose from. You get to these effects by clicking on the FX button on the toolbar on the right side of your workspace. There are appearance type effects as well as motion style effects. It's hard to really demonstrate any of these effects in a book but I will include a couple of screenshots as seen in figures 5.44 and 5.45. You will really need to play with these effects first hand to get an idea of what they do and how they will look.

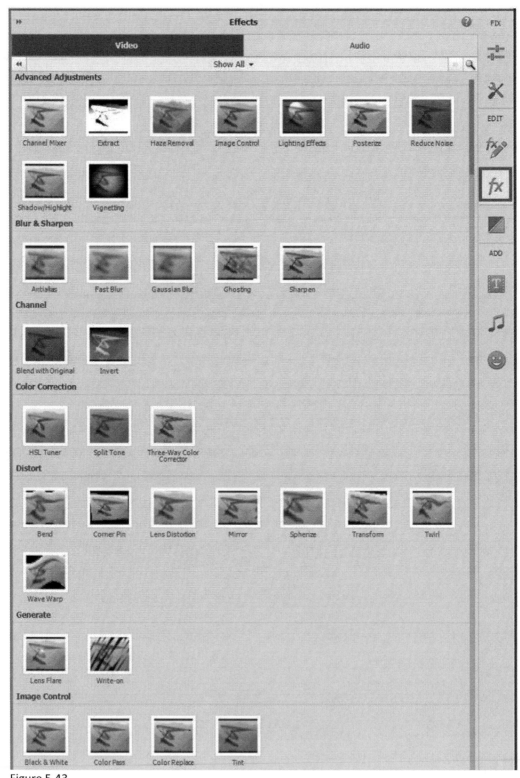

Figure 5.43

Cartoon

Figure 5.44

Lightning

Figure 5.45

Like I mentioned earlier, when you apply many of these effects they will show up in the Applied Effects area allowing you to make adjustments on their settings to fine tune how and when they appear. Figure 5.46 shows a bend effect applied to the clip and figure 5.47 shows the available adjustments for the bend effect.

Figure 5.46

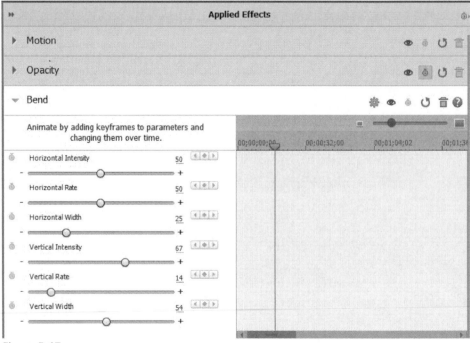

Figure 5.47

If you want to remove an effect from your clip simply click on the trash can icon in the Applied Effects setting or use the *Undo* option from the Edit menu. You can also use the keyboard shortcut Ctrl-Z (Command-Z for Mac) to do the same thing.

As for audio effects, there are not nearly as many as there are for video effects and once again there will be adjustments that you can make in the Applied Effects section once you apply them to a clip. You will need to listen to your audio after applying the effect to see how it affects the sound.

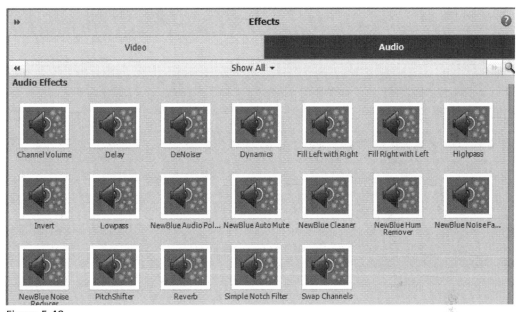

Figure 5.48

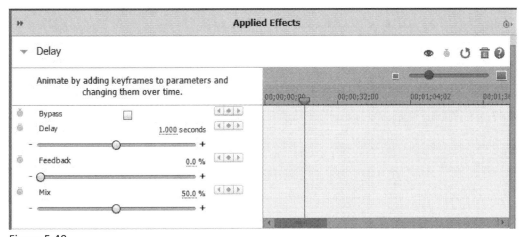

Figure 5.49

When working with these effects, you will see some icons on the toolbar that you should be aware of (figure 5.50).

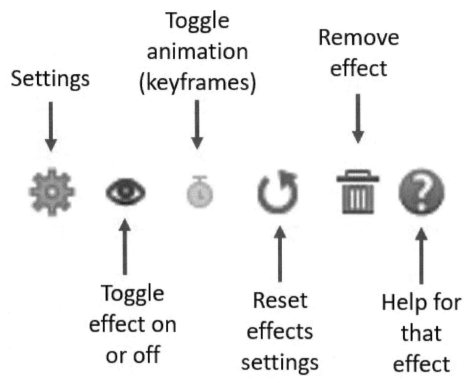

Figure 5.50

When you click on the Settings button for an effect you will get different settings depending on the particular effect.

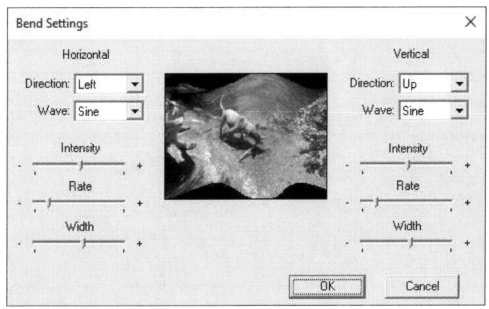

Figure 5.51

Transitions

When your movie consists of many different scenes that tie together, sometimes it's nice to have a custom effect or animation between each scene rather than having them just abruptly go from one to the next. These custom animations are referred to as Transitions and can be applied from the Transition panel that can be accessed right under the Effects button (figure 5.52).

Just like we saw with the Effects, the Transitions are broken down into various categories and there are many to choose from. Plus there are both video and audio transitions that you can use. If you click on a particular transition thumbnail, it will show you a preview within the thumbnail itself.

143

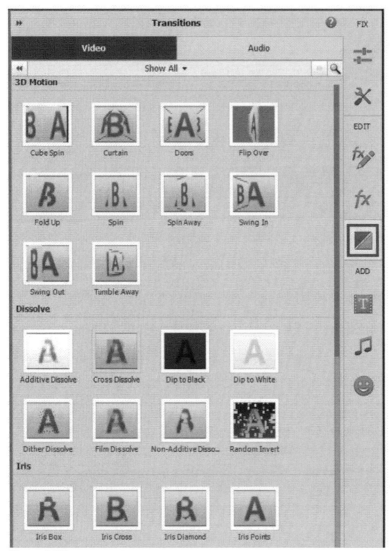

Figure 5.52

Once you decide what transition you want to use, simply drag and drop it on the clip that you want to apply it to. When you drop the transition on the timeline you will be presented with the default duration time that the transition takes which is normally one second.

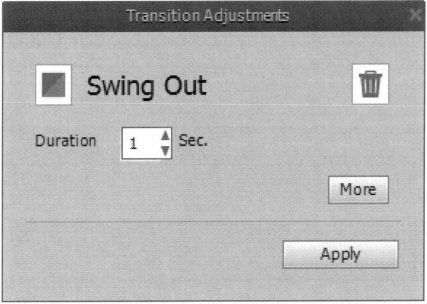

Figure 5.53

Clicking on the More button will give you additional options that you can use to customize how the transition is applied to your clips.

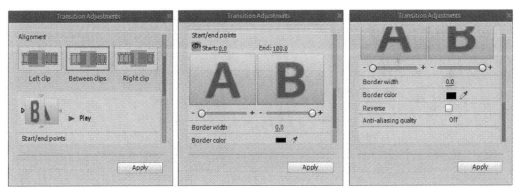

Figure 5.54

The *Alignment* section is important because that tells Premiere where to apply the transition at. You can have it be at the end of the first clip, between both clips or at the beginning of the right clip. Figures 5.55, 5.56 and 5.57 show how the transition looks at each one of these positions on the timeline.

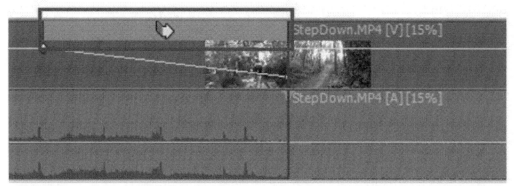

Figure 5.55

Figure 5.56

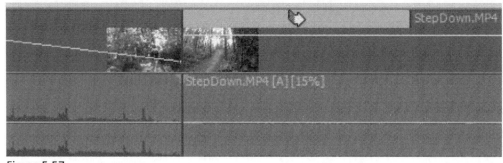

Figure 5.57

You can double click on the transition itself within your clip to bring up the options if you need to make some adjustments. The longer you set the transition to take place for, the larger it will appear within your clip. Figure 5.58 shows how the transition looks when I change it from one to three seconds long.

Figure 5.58

The *Start* and *End* points can be used to determine where the transition effect will begin or end if you don't want to use the default beginning or ending points. In my experience, the defaults work just great.

Figure 5.59

If you want the transition to run backward then simply check the box that says *Reverse* to make this happen. Finally, if you want a border around your transition then you can add one by typing in a number where it says *Border Width* and you can also change the color from the default black if you like.

Once your transition is in place and customized to your liking, all you need to do is play the video to see how it will look in the preview window. If you don't have a very powerful computer then it might not play that smoothly but many times you can render the footage to smooth that out. I will be discussing rendering in Chapter 6.

If you want to remove the transition simply click on it in the timeline and press the delete key on your keyboard or double click it to open up the adjustments window and then click on the trash can icon.

As for audio transitions, Premiere only comes with two of them and they are *Constant Gain* fade and *Constant Power* fade. Constant Gain changes the volume at a constant rate while the Constant Power adds an acceleration or deceleration to the volume in order to make the fade sound less abrupt.

If you want to fade your audio in or out that can be done quite easily on the timeline itself. If you right click on your clip you will see there is a Fade menu option and within there you will have several choices for fading your audio or video in or out. For video fade outs I like to use the Cross Dissolve or Dip to Black effects from the Transitions area.

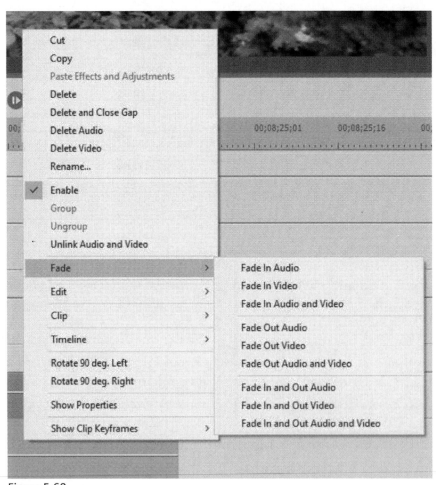

Figure 5.60

To fade out your audio using the Fade options you should first make sure your audio clip is expanded by clicking on the right pointing arrow so you can see the volume indicator line.

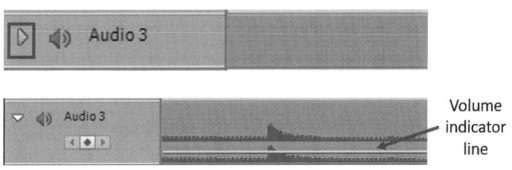

Figure 5.61

You might also want to zoom in closer to the end of the clip so you can get a better view of the volume line for when you need to make your fade out adjustments. You can do this by clicking and dragging on the zoom slider above the timeline. When doing so it's a good idea to place the timeline player line at the point on your clip where you want to zoom into because that's where Premiere will zoom into when you move the slider.

Figure 5.62

Now you can click on *Fade Out Audio* from the Fade right click menu and Premiere will put an anchor on the volume indicator line about one second from the end of the clip. Then it will add a gradual decrease in volume until it gets to the end of the clip.

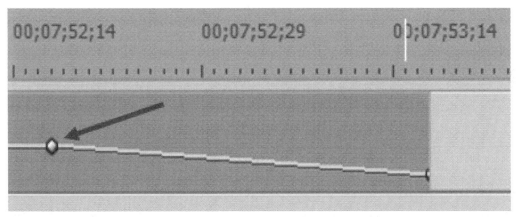

Figure 5.63

If this fade out is not long enough for you then you can drag the anchor to a different location on the clip as shown in figure 5.64.

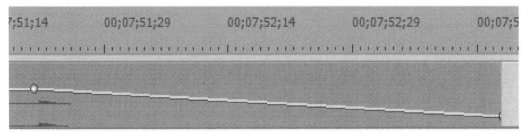

Figure 5.64

Of course, if you want to use the *Fade Out Audio and Video* option to have both faded out at the same time you can use that as well.

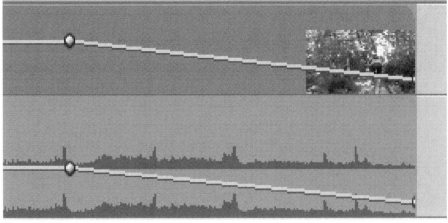

Figure 5.65

 Premiere has the ability to separate the video and audio parts of your video in case you just want to use only one or the other in your movie. This comes in handy if you wanted to do something like copy just the audio portion to be used somewhere else in your project or if you wanted to export just the audio or video part of your project. Simply right click on your clip and choose *Unlink Audio and Video*.

Titles

Titles are a great way to add some introductory text and animations to the beginning of your video or even in the middle to designate a new chapter in your movie. I discussed Title Text back in Chapter 4 and that information pretty much applies to the Titles section that I will be discussing next.

Titles are found right under the Transition section in the ADD group at the right of the Premiere workspace. Just like with all the other components we have seen so far, there are many built in categories to choose from.

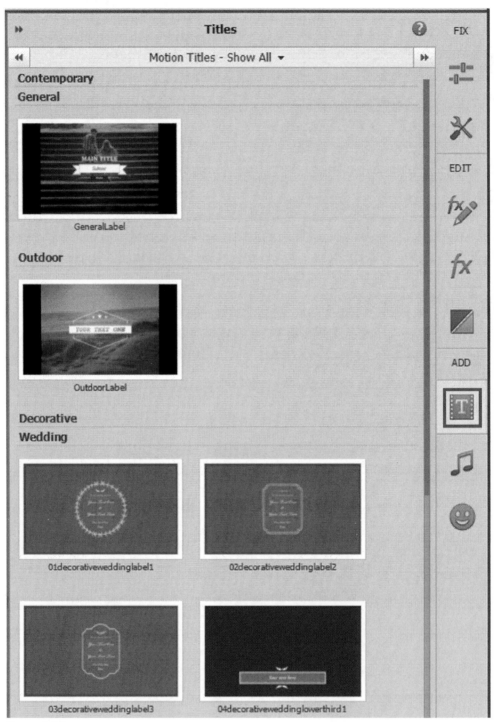

Figure 5.66

Once you choose a Title template, Premiere will download the required files for that template from the Internet so it can be used in your project. Then you just need to edit the text, background and graphic like you did with the other text effects discussed in Chapter 4 and you will have yourself a nice animated text graphic.

Figure 5.67

Graphics

When you want to add some fun to your project you can turn to the Graphics section to find all kinds of colorful cartoons and animations that you can use to enhance and brighten up your video production. You get to the Graphics section by clicking on the smiley face icon in the toolbar to on the right side of the workspace.

The graphics you can choose from are broken down into categories such as Animated Objects, Baby, Costumes, Videos and so on. Some of the graphics are meant to be stationary while others are designed to follow a person or other object throughout the scene and that requires using Motion Tracking that I discussed earlier in this Chapter.

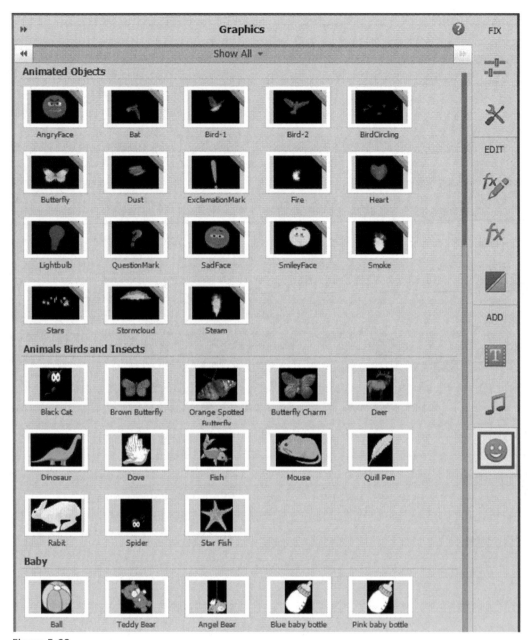

Figure 5.68

Figure 5.69 shows an example of a stationary yet animated graphic where the smiley changes facial expressions during the course of the video. Of course, you can't see that happen so you will have to take my word for it!

Figure 5.70 shows an example of a balloon following the mountain biker as he rides along, and I had to use Motion Tracking to configure this graphic otherwise the balloon would have just stayed in one place.

Figure 5.69

Figure 5.70

Figure 5.71 shows some stationary graphics placed on a still image of some dogs
that can be used as an introductory image for something like a dog birthday party

video. If I were to have placed these graphics on a moving video then as the dogs moved the speech bubble, party hat, flower and cake would have stayed in the same place while the dogs moved around.

Figure 5.71

Now that you have an idea of how these video enhancement tools work you should take some time and play around with them to get the hang of them since reading about them only does so much good when it comes to understanding how they work.

Chapter 6 - Exporting and Sharing Your Video

If you spend hours editing and customizing your videos to make them worthy of a red carpet premiere then what's the point of doing all that work if you can't share them with others? Isn't that the whole point of using video editing software like Premiere?

Fortunately, the exporting and sharing process is much easier than the editing process and in most cases doesn't take nearly as long to accomplish. Before you decide how you are going to finalize your movie you need to figure out what you are going to do with it. Are you going to burn it to a DVD to watch at home? Are you going to upload it to YouTube to share with the world? Or maybe you are going to post it on your own website.

This decision will determine how you export your final movie. But the good thing is that you are not stuck with only one choice. As long as you save your project and its related files, you can export and share it differently later on if needed. Just keep in mind that saving your projects and their files can take up a lot of space on your computer so plan ahead.

What Type of File Should I Export My Video As?

One nice feature of Premiere Elements is that it will choose the best file type for your movie based on the export settings that you choose. For example, if you are going to export your movie to be burned to a DVD then it will choose the *MPEG2-DVD* format for you, so you don't need to figure it out for yourself. Or if you were to choose the YouTube export option it would use the *H.264* file type since that's what most people use for their YouTube videos.

In general, you are fine sticking with the suggested file types when doing an export based on what you plan on using your video for. Later in the chapter, I will be discussing how you can do a custom export and choose your own file type for your export as well as change additional settings such as the frame rate and video size.

Rendering Your Project

You might recall that I have mentioned the word render a few times in this book. Now that I have covered all the basics and you hopefully have a good idea of what you need to do in order to edit your movie to your liking, it's now time to finalize it before exporting it.

Rendering is when Premiere takes all of the components of your project such as video, audio, music, pictures, graphics, etc. and combines them into an actual video rather than a bunch of separate parts. This is required to make everything run smoothly together for the best overall results.

You don't have to render your video before exporting it but for the most part it won't come out as well as if you do. Even though I am discussing rendering near the end of the book doesn't mean you have to wait until then either. You can render your project whenever you like and as often as you like.

Once you render your project it will stay rendered and you won't have to do it again unless you make any changes that need to be re-rendered. Then when you go to render your project again, only those changes will need to be rendered (most of the time).

If you look at the top of your timeline you will see an orange colored line as shown in figure 6.1 within the dashed line box.

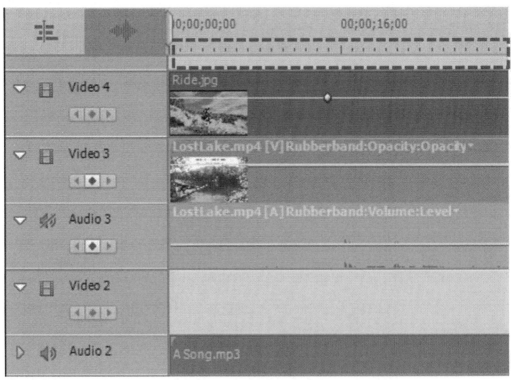

Figure 6.1

This means that this section of the project has not been rendered. If the line were green then you know the rendering process has been applied to the project or at least to that part of the project. As you add more media to your timeline you will see that the part of the timeline with the new media will be orange while the rendered part of the timeline will stay green. Then when you click the Render button again, the green section will go by really fast and then slow down when it gets to the orange section.

Before you render you need to make sure that you have the part of the timeline you want to be rendered selected. At the top of the timeline where the time markers are there is a slider that is used to designate which part of your timeline you want to have rendered (and also exported when the time comes). If you hover your mouse over this slider it will tell you the start point, end point and duration of what will be rendered or exported as seen in figure 6.2. You can move this slider in either direction to set the proper start and end points for your video.

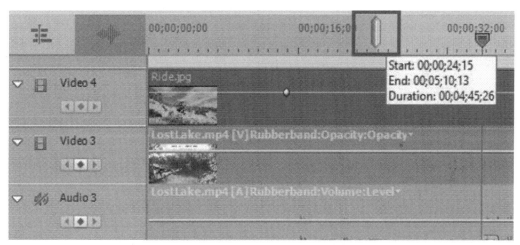

Figure 6.2

There is also another slider that can be used if you want to render or export a part of your timeline that is in the middle rather than starting from the end. In that case, you can position them where you would like the start and end points to be as seen in figure 6.3.

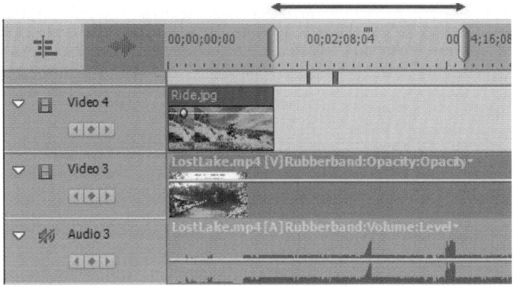

Figure 6.3

When everything is looking the way you like, and you have the video duration slider in place then it's time to click on the *Render* button and wait for the process to complete. The Render button is located above the timeline and below the preview screen. This process will take some time and is dependent on how long your video is, how many media items you have in your project and the performance level of your computer. When you start the process you will see a progress bar that tells you how many frames it is rendering, and the approximate time left to completion.

Rendering   ✕

Progress

Rendering 1 of 4 Video Previews

[███──────────────────────────] 13%

Rendering frame 337 of 2565

Estimated Time Left: 0:01:22

▶ Render Details

Cancel

Figure 6.4

Once the render is complete I would save my project and then get ready to export my final movie using one of the many export options which I will discuss next.

Quick Export

The Quick Export option can be used to export your video in a format that can be viewed on most commonly used devices such as smartphones, tablets, computers and websites. It will export your video as an MP4 file which is a very common video file type.

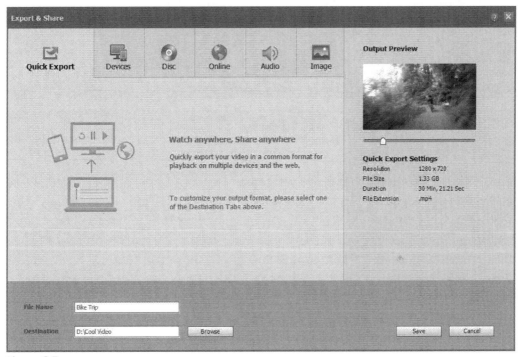

Figure 6.5

It will use a resolution based on your source media files so in my case it will export the movie at a 1280x720 resolution (720p). Your videos will most likely be 1080p but since I had some older footage in my project it used the 720p settings.

The *File Size* section tells you how large of a file you will end up with after you export your project to a video file. This way you will have an idea if it will fit on something like a flash drive, CD\DVD or if it will take a long time to upload to a site like YouTube.

The *Duration* section tells you how long your movie will be which you can also see on your project timeline.

When you look at an actual video file on your computer, it will have a thumbnail preview that shows you a frame from the actual video as shown in figure 6.6.

StepDown.MP4

Figure 6.6

The *Output Preview* slider can be used to choose what frame of your video will be shown in video previews so it's a good idea to choose a frame of your video that highlights what the movie is about. When uploading your video to video sites it will also sometimes use the video's preview selection. I have found that this is a hit or miss feature since sometimes it doesn't show the frame I have chosen depending on the situation, but it doesn't hurt to find a preview that you like.

Before you export your video you will need to choose a location on your computer to export the video to. You will need to make sure that location has enough free space to store the video as well. The *Destination* box shows where the video will be exported to and if you want to change that location, simply click on the *Browse* button and navigate to a new location. Next, you need to type in a file name for the video before saving it. This name has nothing to do with what will show on your video but is only used to name the actual file itself.

Export for Devices

Next on the list of export options is the Export for Devices section. Here you will have many different choices for a variety of different devices. As you can see in figure 6.7 there are options for Computer, TV, Mobile and Custom and each option has different settings that will be used when exporting your movie.

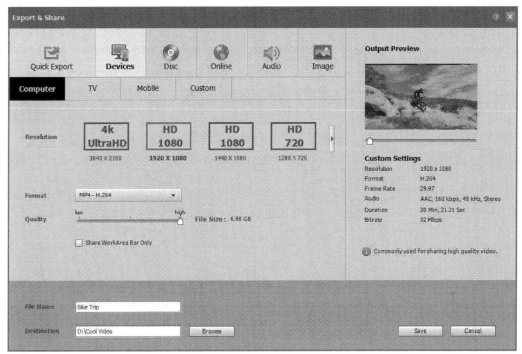

Figure 6.7

For the *Computer* options, you have various choices for video resolution as well as other options for the format based on what resolution you choose. I always like to choose the resolution based on the actual resolution of the original footage I used for my project. Sure you can export a 1080p project using the 4k settings but that doesn't mean it will make your 1080p footage magically have the same quality as actual 4k footage.

The *Format* dropdown will have different choices based on the resolution you use such as MP4, MPEG, AVI, MOV, WMV and so on. When you chose a resolution it will show you the settings it will be using for the export under the *Custom Settings* section on the right.

The *Quality* slider bar can be used to increase the overall quality of your exported movie based on where you position the slider. You will notice as you move the slider to the right to increase the quality, the file size will increase as well.

If you only want to export a certain part of your project then you can select that part using the slider markers as shown back in figure 6.3 and check the box that says *Share WorkArea Bar Only*.

Figure 6.8 shows the export options for *TV* and figure 6.9 shows the export settings for *Mobile* devices. You might have noticed that the file size for each device type varies quite a bit which tells you that the overall quality for each type will vary.

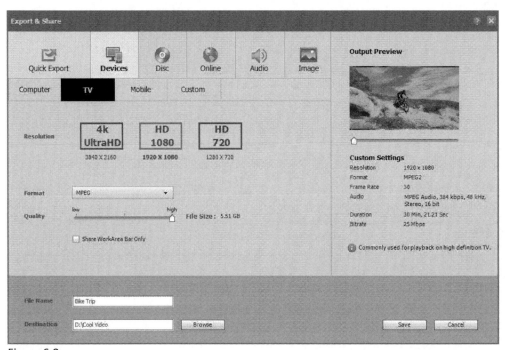

Figure 6.8

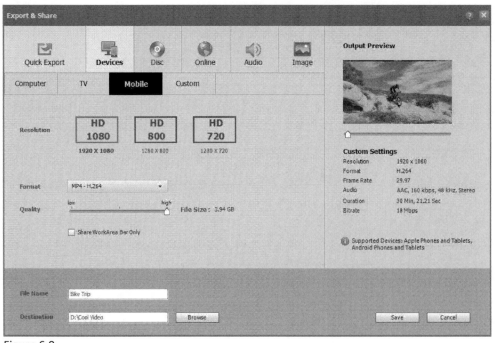

Figure 6.9

I didn't include any images for the *Custom* settings because I will be going over that later in the chapter.

Burn to Disk

Many people like to put their movies on a DVD or Blu Ray disk so they can watch them on their TVs or bring them to other places to easily watch using DVD\Blu Ray players.

You don't have as many options when burning to disk and the settings will vary depending on what kind of drive(s) you have installed in your computer. The burn to disk screen will still look very similar to the burn to devices screen from the previous section.

You will have two choices when it comes to the process of burning your movie to a DVD and it's all up to you as to which method you choose. If you want to first burn the movie to a file on your computer and then later burn it to disk then you can choose the *ISO Image* under the Type options. This will create an ISO (International Organization for Standardization) file which contains all of the data for your movie in a single file. Then you can use your favorite CD burning software to burn the contents of this ISO file on to a DVD that you can then watch using your home DVD player. You can then make additional copies of your movie on other DVDs by burning the file to disk as many times as needed.

Figure 6.10 shows the burn to disk settings and at the bottom under type, I have chosen ISO Image (4.7 GB) for a standard DVD. There is also an 8.5 GB options for dual-sided DVD disks that will hold more data.

The checkbox that says Fit Contents to available space is used to ensure that your entire project will fit on the disk size that you are using. It might sacrifice a little quality to make it all fit, but this is usually better than not having enough space on your disk to fit the whole movie.

Also, make sure you have enough free space on your computer in the location shown under *Destination* otherwise you will need to choose a different location.

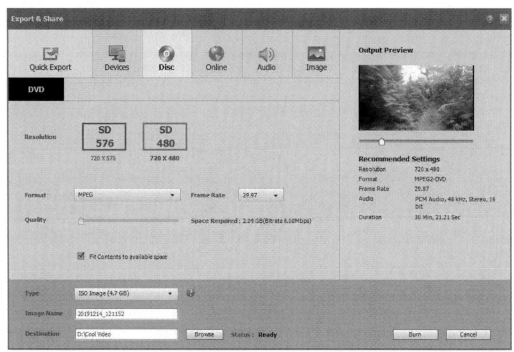

Figure 6.10

If you would rather burn your project directly to your DVD or Blu Ray disk than you can choose the *Disk* option under Type (figure 6.11) rather than the ISO option. For the Destination you will need to select your computer's DVD drive. After that, simply insert a blank disk into your DVD\Blu Ray drive and then click on the *Burn* button to start the process.

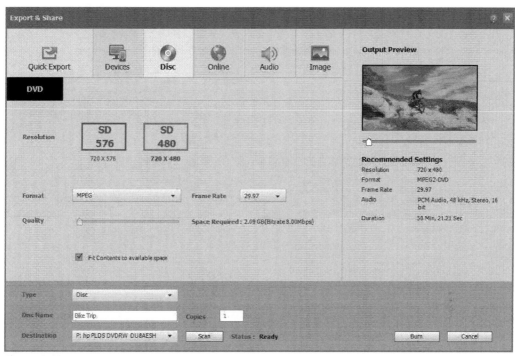

Figure 6.11

Uploading Your Video to be Used Online

If you are like many people and are into posting your movies on video sharing sites such as YouTube then you might want to use the *Online* export method to make sure that your movies look their best when posted on these types of sites.

Premiere Elements offers built in export settings for YouTube as well as Vimeo so that you can easily export your videos, so they are ready to go for these types of video sharing sites.

Once you choose your resolution and quality settings you can simply click on the Begin Share button as seen in figure 6.12 to have Premiere export your video to one of the two supported sharing sites.

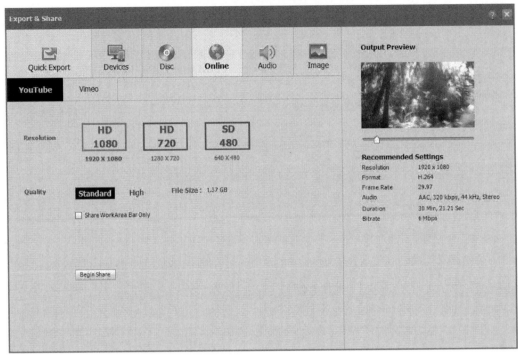

Figure 6.12

You will most likely need to sign in to your YouTube or Vimeo account the first time before being able to export your video.

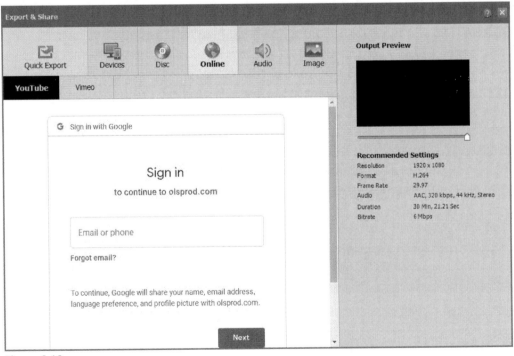

Figure 6.13

Unfortunately, when it comes to YouTube (owned by Google) access, they seem to have an issue with allowing Premiere access to their site to upload your videos directly to it. I have reached out to Adobe to see if they had a solution but apparently its too much effort on their part to get someone to respond.

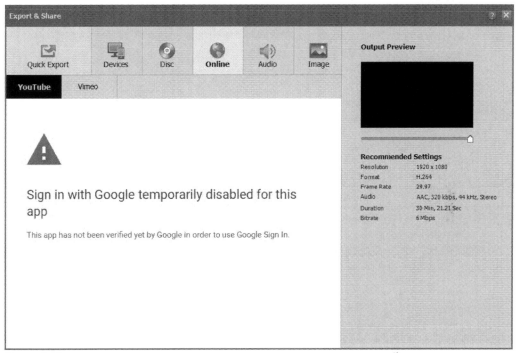

Figure 6.14

Hopefully, by the time you are reading this, they will have the issue fixed or maybe your version will work better when it comes to connecting to YouTube to directly upload your videos!

Regardless, you can still use one of the other options to export your video and then manually upload it to your YouTube account. I like to use the Computer export settings with the quality set to high under Devices for my YouTube videos.

Custom Export
If you happen to have experience with video formats, codecs, frame rates and other aspects of video files then you might want to use the Custom Export setting to create your own custom settings that you can use to export your movies, so they look their best for your particular application.

For most beginners and even novice users, you might not ever have a need to create your own custom settings since the choices from the other export types work quite well for the most part. Since this is not an advanced Premiere book I will just briefly go over this section and show you the settings you can change here.

When you first go to the Custom export options you will notice that you don't have any custom presets configured. If you click on the *Advanced Settings* button then you will be able to create your own custom preset that you can then use whenever you need when those custom settings apply to a video project you are exporting.

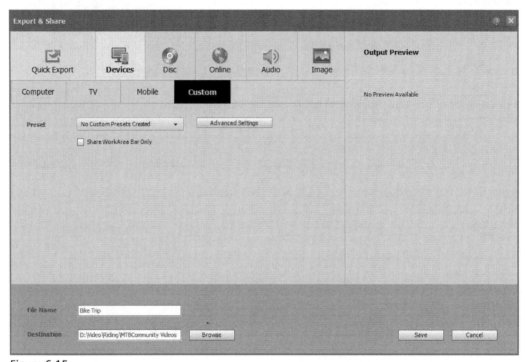

Figure 6.15

Figure 6.16 shows the settings that can be configured for the H.264 video format. As you can see, there are many different settings to choose from and you kind of need to know what you are doing if you plan on changing any of these settings. If you choose a different format then the available settings will be different as well.

Many times you will be doing some research online about how to export a certain type of video and you will read about which settings need to be changed for the best results and then you can come here and see if you can find the settings that you need to change.

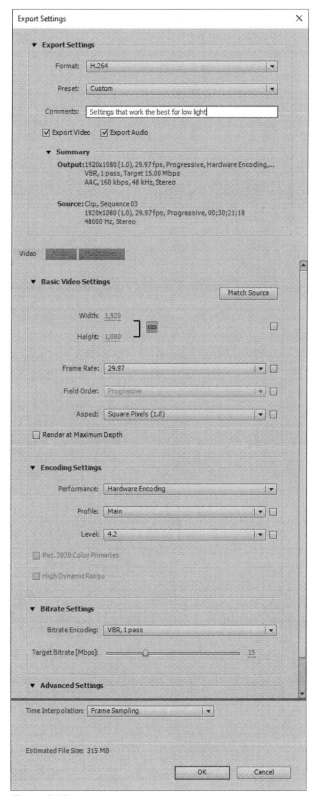

Figure 6.16

Once you configure the settings to your liking, you can click on the OK button to save the preset with a name of your choosing.

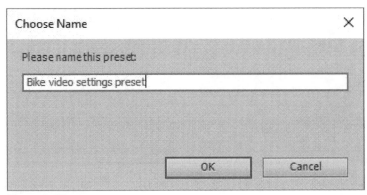

Figure 6.17

Then when you go back to the Custom export settings, you will see your saved preset there and then you can export your project/video using those custom settings. If you want to remove that preset then simply click the trash can icon to the right of the preset name.

Figure 6.18

Exporting Audio Only

There may be a time when you only want to export the audio portion of your project rather than both the audio and video. For example, let's say you recorded a music concert and want to make an audio cd of just the music and don't need the video.

To do this simply go to the Audio export section and choose your file type and quality level. Then you will need to give the file a name and choose an export location just like you did when exporting your videos.

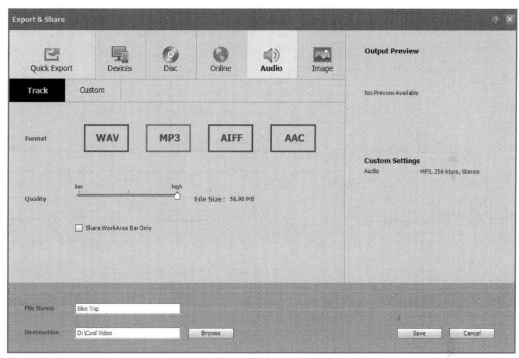

Figure 6.19

Just like with the video settings, there are custom export settings for audio files as well that you can access from the *Custom* tab. Then you can adjust the settings to suit your needs (figure 6.20) and save the preset to be used again in the future.

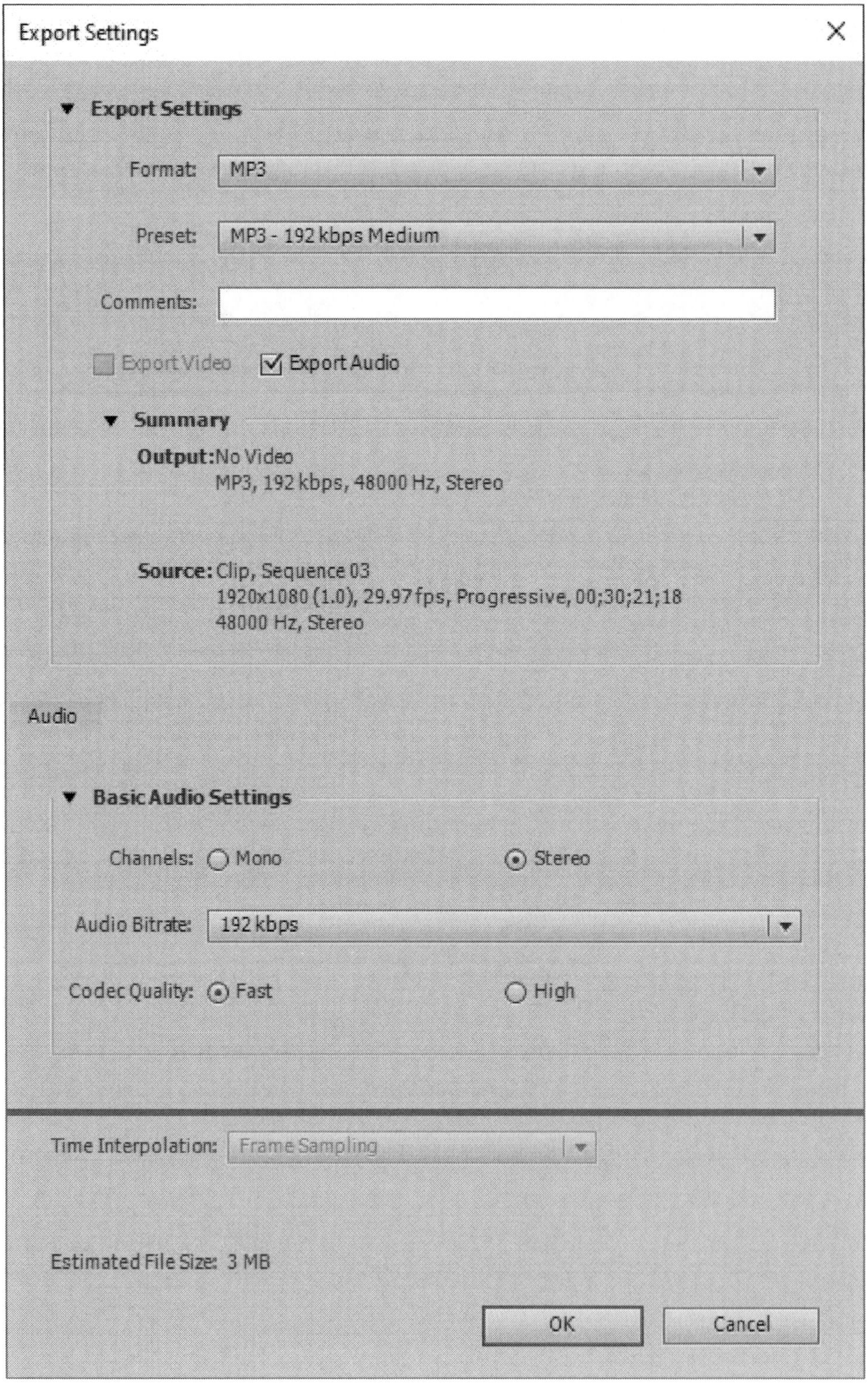

Export Settings   ✕

▼ **Export Settings**

Format: MP3 ▾

Preset: MP3 - 192 kbps Medium ▾

Comments: [ ]

☐ Export Video   ☑ Export Audio

▼ **Summary**

Output: No Video
    MP3, 192 kbps, 48000 Hz, Stereo

Source: Clip, Sequence 03
    1920x1080 (1.0), 29.97 fps, Progressive, 00;30;21;18
    48000 Hz, Stereo

Audio

▼ **Basic Audio Settings**

Channels: ◯ Mono   ◉ Stereo

Audio Bitrate: 192 kbps ▾

Codec Quality: ◉ Fast   ◯ High

Time Interpolation: Frame Sampling ▾

Estimated File Size: 3 MB

    OK   Cancel

Figure 6.20

Exporting a Frame as an Image

The final export process I will be going over involves taking a specific frame of your video and exporting it as an image file. There are a couple of ways to do this and the first way is by choosing the *Frame* option under the *Image* export section. When using this method you first need to pause your video on your timeline at the exact frame you wish to export to an image file. Once you are on the right location on your timeline then you can go to Export and it should show that same frame in your Output Preview window as seen in figure 6.21.

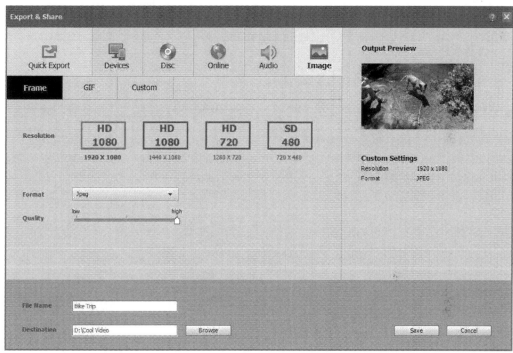

Figure 6.21

Then all you need to do once again is give it a name and choose a location to save the image file in and click on the *Save* button. Premiere will then export that frame as a jpeg image file.

Using the GIF option will create what is called an animated GIF file which is technically an animated image file that uses a select group of frames to appear as a small movie. Think of it as when you were a kid and made animated characters in a notebook by putting small changes on each page and then flipped through the pages really quickly to make it look like the character was moving.

When using the GIF option you will notice that the box that says *Show WorkArea Bar Only* is checked because that is where Premiere will be taking the frames to create the animated image file. So if you use your entire timeline without designating a small area instead then you will end up with a huge image file that you really won't be able to use for anything. In fact, it even has a message at the bottom of the export screen that says, "To get the best results, recommended GIF duration is 5-10 seconds".

Not all image viewing programs will be able to show the animations for animated GIF files so if you double click your exported GIF file and nothing happens then that is most likely the case. You can usually open GIF files with your web browser and it will then show the animations.

Now that you know how to export your videos and are familiar with all of the various export options you have at your disposal, take some time and export your project using different settings to see how the results will vary and hopefully you will find the perfect settings to get the professional look you are "shooting" for!

What's Next?

Now that you have read through this book and taken your video editing skills to the next level, you might be wondering what you should do next. Well, that depends on where you want to go. Are you happy with what you have learned, or do you want to further your knowledge on Elements or even give Premiere CC a try to see if you can make some even more professional looking movies?

If you do want to expand your knowledge, then you can look for some more advanced books on Elements or ones that cover Premiere CC itself, if that's the path you choose to follow. Focus on mastering the basics, and then apply what you have learned when going to more advanced material.

There are many great video resources as well, such as Pluralsight or CBT Nuggets, which offer online subscriptions to training videos of every type imaginable. YouTube is also a great source for instructional videos if you know what to search for.

If you are content in being a proficient Elements user that knows more than your friends, then just keep on practicing what you have learned. Don't be afraid to poke around with some of the settings and tools that you normally don't use and see if you can figure out what they do without having to research it since learning by doing is the most effective method to gain new skills.

Thanks for reading **Premiere Elements Made Easy**. You can also check out the other books in the Made Easy series for additional computer related information and training. You can get more information on my other books on my Computers Made Easy Book Series website.

https://www.madeeasybookseries.com/

You should also check out my computer tips website, as well as follow it on Facebook to find more information on all kinds of computer topics.

www.onlinecomputertips.com
https://www.facebook.com/OnlineComputerTips/

About the Author

James Bernstein has been working with various companies in the IT field since 2000, managing technologies such as SAN and NAS storage, VMware, backups, Windows Servers, Active Directory, DNS, DHCP, Networking, Microsoft Office, Photoshop, Premiere, Exchange, and more.

He has obtained certifications from Microsoft, VMware, CompTIA, ShoreTel, and SNIA, and continues to strive to learn new technologies to further his knowledge on a variety of subjects.

He is also the founder of the website onlinecomputertips.com, which offers its readers valuable information on topics such as Windows, networking, hardware, software, and troubleshooting. James writes much of the content himself and adds new content on a regular basis. The site was started in 2005 and is still going strong today.

Made in the USA
Middletown, DE
22 March 2021